Finding Your Bootstraps: 11 Steps to Overcoming Victim Thinking

To Joey   8-1-15

You can do it!!
Find your bootstraps & just

Diane Bogino

Keep pulling!

Diane Bogid

ISBN 978-0-9772724-0-2
Library of Congress: 2005933201

Editor and Layout: M. Kay duPont

Printed and manufactured in the United States of America.

Published by Gerald Simmons & Associates, Atlanta, GA

For more information or to order more books,
visit www.performstrat.com/boots.html

FOREWORD

I've known Diane Bogino for many years, in several arenas: On the personal side, it's my pleasure to call her "friend." On the business side, I've been her editor since she took the big, fearsome leap into authorhood with her first adult book; I've been her associate in the speaking world; and I've been her partner on several projects. No matter how much I see her, she never ceases to amaze me with her energy, her humor, her love for life, and her beauty.

Now, with this book, I've learned things about her early life that I never imagined. It's hard for me to see how a child could live through the events in this book and grow up to be such a warm, trusting woman.

But this is not just another book about the tragedies of life and overcoming abuse. It's a book about *doing* it for yourself. We all have problems to master—some of us are still in the situations and some of us live with the memories. *Finding Your Bootstraps* gives all of us 11 believable, doable steps to finding our voice and our place. Will it be easy? No, and Diane doesn't sugarcoat that. But someone has finally written a book for the layperson who just wants to know how to get on with his or her life—and that person is Diane Bogino. Thank you, Diane!

—M. Kay duPont, CSP, CPDT

Author of five books, including *Don't Let Your Participles Dangle in Public!* and *Writing for the College-Bound Student (and Anyone Else Who Needs to Revise, Review or Refresh).*

Acknowledgments

Thank you to my loving husband for his support, encouragement and understanding. His patience, gentle spirit and kindness have been a wonderful inspiration. And, yes, he STILL brings me breakfast in bed every morning. A special thanks to his loving family for believing I could make this special man happy.

Thank you to my daughter Brittany, my son Bobby and my grandson Nathan for believing in me and for putting up with all the times my silly sense of humor has embarrassed them in public. Congratulations to Brittany and my new son-in-law, Wayne Newberry.

Thank you to Wayne Newberry for the cover design.

Thank you to my editor, M. Kay duPont. She can breath life into words, bring understanding to ideas, and put any wild and wooly punctuation in its place. Every good book needs a good editor and Kay is one of the best!

Thank you to everyone who has allowed me to use their material and quotes.

And a special thank you to Robert A. Yourell, LMFT, for his generous spirit and sound advice.

Table of Contents

To Mother

A life missed…then and now.

Introduction

"Come on! Pull yourself up by your bootstraps!" That's what people used to say when someone was down or experiencing hard times. There was no therapy, no coaching and no crying on your best friend's shoulder. You just coped. You just pulled on those old bootstraps. But, as a wise friend of mine once said, "People tell me to pull myself up by the bootstraps, but no one tells me where to buy the bootstraps!"

The good news is that you don't have to buy the bootstraps at all. Or borrow them, or even rent them. Your bootstraps are with you all the time, and you can pull them up from deep inside your own being. Some people may have longer or stronger internal straps, but even if yours are threadbare, you can do a little repair work to make them more substantial and effective! The power is already in you! Your bootstraps are built in and just waiting for that first tug! GO FOR IT!

All the powers in the universe are already ours. It is we who have put our hands before our eyes and cry that it is dark.

~~Swami Vivekananda (1863-1904)
Indian monk and spiritual philosopher

According to the book *Psychology, an Introduction, Sixth Edition,* by Charles G. Morris, "Motives and emotions both energize and direct our

2

behavior. The two are closely related and can activate us even without our awareness. Motives are triggered by bodily needs, cues in the environment, and such feelings as loneliness or guilt. When such stimuli combine to create a motive, goal-directed behavior results. Like motives, emotions—which usually refer to such complex feelings as anger, fear or love—activate behavior, but it is more difficult to predict the behavior and goals affected by emotion than those stimulated by motives.

Emotions, like motives, arouse and direct our behavior. We can classify emotions in terms of whether they cause us to avoid something (fear), approach something aggressively (anger), or approach something with acceptance (joy, love). Emotions can either help or hinder performance. The Yerkes-Dodson law states that the more complex the task, the lower the level of emotional arousal that can be tolerated before performance declines."

The question is: How much are you willing to adapt your behavior to have the life you want? In other words, how much are you inclined to change in order to reach the performance you need to fulfill your goals? Are you willing to change your environment—leave a bad relationship, avoid negative people, switch jobs? Are you amenable to changing your lifestyle—to give up the boredom or the drama, stop chasing the excitement, perform the daily tasks necessary to reach your goals? How much courage are you prepared to put forth? Can you give up the fear of rejection or not being good enough?

To climb steep hills requires slow pace at first.
~~William Shakespeare (1564-1616)
Elizabethan playwright

Change takes time and it's painful on several levels. (If it were easy, everyone would be changing their behavior to achieve success.) You'll have to learn to be patient with yourself. Sometimes it's difficult for people to reach deep inside themselves and work past all the pain, all the road blocks, all the guilt, all the trash that's preventing them from finding their bootstraps. The good news is that you CAN do it!

This book will help you overcome victim thinking so you can make your life more successful and productive. The 11 steps we'll discuss helped me get back to sanity, throw away my "victim" crutches, and live an enjoyable life, and they can help you too. It doesn't matter where you start from, only that you start! Whether you're eighteen or eighty, you have no more excuses!

Youth is not a time of life, it is a state of mind. You are as old as your doubt, your fear, your despair. The way to keep young is to keep your faith young. Keep your self-confidence young. Keep your hope young.

~~Luella F. Phean

My Early Life—
Hang On, Sloopy, Hang On

Bootstrap: noun: A strap that is looped and sewn to the top of a boot for pulling it on

verb: (bootstraping, bootstrapped): To help oneself, often through improvished means.

I didn't even know I had bootstraps, much less where they were or how to pull myself up on them. During most of my life's journey, I lived in the sewer of depression, a gutter without self-confidence, self-respect or self-knowledge. Internal hate had almost devoured my soul. We'll start at one of the darkest stops on my journey.

My knuckles were white from gripping the kitchen counter so tightly. In my mind, all I had to do was to walk back to the bedroom, get the gun out of the closet, put the barrel to my temple, pull the trigger, and it would all be over. Sweet peace. No more nightmares. No more thoughts of my childhood. No more feelings of inadequacy. No more horrible feelings of never being good enough, smart enough, pretty enough. No more façade relationships. Death—a serene escape that would stop the sadness and pain that no one else could see.

As you might imagine, the road to this decision was littered with shattered dreams. I was born into a tragically dysfunctional family. But at the time, the 1940s, no one had ever heard of a "dysfunctional" family. Everybody's business was their own.

The first house I remember living in was a small, one-bedroom duplex. My two older brothers shared the enclosed back porch as a bedroom. I slept in the same bed with my parents. My father was a house painter, my mother a housewife.

The one pleasant memory I have is of playing Little Miss Muffet in the first grade. Other memories of that time are less enjoyable: having jaundice and watching the doctor stomp out of my hospital room because I wouldn't let him put needles into my ankles; my mother yanking my hair while combing it and yelling at me for crying; waking up on the sofa in our house one night with some man—I have no idea who—trying to fondle me.

I remember coming out of a bar with my mother one night and getting into a car with two men. (I don't know if one was my father or not.) They were drunk and we promptly backed into a telephone pole.

I remember going with my mother to her lover's house. They went into the bedroom and left me alone with my hands over my ears.

I remember walking home from school one day and imitating two male schoolmates who were on the other side of the street. They failed to see the humor. One came across the street and punched me in the stomach. Ouch! My mother paid a visit to their mother, however, and I don't remember the boys bothering me again. At least not *those* boys.

Here is my family before my brothers and I were taken away
and placed in foster welfare homes:
Mother: Agnes Lucile Johnston Steen (Deceased)
Brother: Matthew Kenneth (Kenny) Steen, Jr.
Me: Diane Elizabeth Steen Bogino
Brother: Gerard (Gerry) Michael Steen (Deceased)
Father: Matthew Kenneth Steen, Sr. (Deceased)

Uncle Harry, Aunt Janie and me.
(This is the aunt and uncle who raised
me from the age of 10 to 18.)

Here's John and me "cookin' something up" in Provino's Italian Restaurant

My daughter, Brittany, and her new husband, Wayne Newberry.

My son, Bob Bogino, and my daughter, Brittany. This picture was taken at Scalini's on Cobb Parkway in Smyrna, GA.

One day my brothers and I were playing in an abandoned building in a shopping center when my older brother found some matches. When the fire began, my other brother and I decided we didn't want any part of it, so we struck out for home as fast as our little legs would carry us. As we ran, we saw police cars heading to the "scene of the crime" with their lights flashing. When we saw fire trucks rushing by with their sirens blaring, we became even more frightened. When we reached home, we raced up the front steps, across the porch, through the living room where our father and aunt were "resting," through the kitchen, and out the back door. As we sat on the steps and caught our breath, my 10-year-old brother, being more experienced and worldly, put his arm around me and said, "Don't worry about a thing, kid. They'll never find us here."

I think that's the last time I ever listened to anything **he** had to say. In about 30 minutes, we heard the clomp of heavy shoes coming up the front steps, across the porch, through the living room where our father and aunt were still passed out in their drunken stupor, through the kitchen, and out to the steps where we sat. They had my 11-year-old brother with them.

While all of this was going on, my mother was on her way home from the hospital where they had patched her up from a fight she and my father had had earlier that day. When she saw the police, she decided not to go to the house. I don't know where she went, but she didn't go home! That very day, my brothers and I were taken away from our parents and placed in a foster welfare home. As I remember, I slept in an attic space. I pretended that it meant I was destined to go right to the top!

There were several other children of varying ages in that first foster home. One was a boy a couple of years older than I. He liked to play doctor, and guess who his favorite patient was? The foster parents must have found about it because they sat me down and asked, "Don't you want to be a nice little girl?" Well, sure I did. I often still wonder if anyone asked the boy, "Don't you want to be a nice little boy?" But I seriously doubt that happened. My brothers and I were then separated—they were sent to another home together and I was sent to a different place.

My second "family" consisted of a mother, father and three teenaged boys. OK, ten guesses, what's wrong with *that* picture? Yep, you guessed it. All three of the boys molested me. One day I finally got up the courage to tell the foster mother what had been going on and that I had been injured. (Seeing blood had scared the pants off me. No pun intended. Well, maybe a little one.)

She asked me which of her sons had been doing these things and I said all of them. Her middle son was her favorite and she couldn't even entertain the thought that this little angel could possibly be involved in such lurid activities, so she began to threaten *me*: "You'd better be telling the truth, because when he comes home, I'm going to ask him, and if you're lying, I'll beat you to a pulp."

I figured this kid was going to lie his little heart out anyway, so I said, "No, it wasn't him." She pushed me against the wall, put her cigarette out in the kitchen sink (a real class act), and made good on her promise to beat me. I thought my short life was over, and I vowed to always tell the truth from that point forward, no matter what the consequences—providing, of course, that I made it out of the kitchen with all my limbs still attached!

When the boys came home, she gently comforted her son in the back yard, and I heard her say, "Haven't I told you before about doing this?" Apparently I was not their first victim. I don't know whether I was their last victim, because one of the foster mother's young female relatives came and took me on her bike to her house. As she told her mother how badly I was being beaten, the radio was playing "Your Cheating Heart." Man, I thought, you're telling me!

Apparently these women called the authorities (bless them) and I was sent to another home in a middle-class neighborhood. This one was clean and well kept, and the parents were middle-aged, upstanding citizens. Even though the foster father must have made a decent salary as an engineer in an aircraft-manufacturing plant, I had only two dresses to wear to school. They were the same style—plaid cotton with a bibbed collar edged in cotton lace. One had more green in it, the other had more red. (Yes, I have a clothes habit today.)

The foster father did see that I was well educated, however— well educated in how to please a man sexually. And three guesses about whom I was pleasing.

11

One day, when I was 8 or 9, the foster mother went to the grocery store and came back sooner than expected. She found her husband (my foster father) on top of me on the floor. She asked, "What are you doing?"

He replied, "I'm kissing her, June, what does it look like I'm doing?" June simply left the room. He continued to abuse me the entire time I was in their home, from second grade through fourth grade.

During this time, I was also molested by a couple of boys at school. One of them was quite older than I—a counselor at the school's summer day camp. The other was a fourth-grade classmate. Fourth grade! Talk about a well-rounded education.

In all these years, our real parents never tried to get any of us kids back, but they did continue their drinking and fighting. After their final battle, my father wound up dead and my mother was sent to prison. One of my relatives attended her trial (none of us children attended) and later told me that the judge stated right before he sentenced her, "This is the worst travesty of justice I have ever seen." Spousal abuse was looked at differently in those days. To this day, my oldest brother cannot forgive my mother. He now has a website that supposedly functions as a source for some genealogical information and on it he states that the cause of my father's death was "murder." In my mother's defense, I have never believed that she intentionally caused my father's death. I will always believe that it was just a horrible accident. I believe the website statement is just my brother's way of getting the "last laugh" or "punishing" my mother, even though she is no longer around to defend herself.

When my mother had cancer, he initially took care of her. According to my mother, who was not known to lie, he would not even allow her to have her purse. He would taunt her and say, "You don't need this, you're going to die!" There were other, more serious, accusations lodged, however, nothing was ever proven on either side. At any rate, I wound up taking care of my mother during her last days. She wrote a will and left me her small inheritance. From a portion of the total, I gave equal amounts of money to each of her seven grandchildren.

But I digress. Back to the trial: Mother was sentenced to five years and off she went. I remember that she worked in the prison nursery, because I once had a picture of her holding an infant there. Funny, isn't it? She didn't take care of her own kids, but she ended up taking care of kids she didn't know.

After my mother was sentenced, the State asked, "Now what are we supposed to do with this little girl?" They wanted to put me up for adoption, and the foster parents I lived with considered it. I was terrified! Instead, my elderly great aunt and uncle decided they would take me to live with them. I met them one night and was shortly thereafter put on an airplane (my first flight) all by myself, to go to a city I had never seen, to spend the rest of my life with two people I had only met once.

The good news is that the abuse stopped. The bad news is that I was in for a culture shock. The house my aunt and uncle lived in was on an unpaved street, it had an outhouse, the wringer-style washing machine was on the back porch, and my bedroom was actually a sun porch. This room had no insulation and, in the winter, there would be sheets of ice on the walls!

My aunt and uncle were devoutly religious and extremely strict. I was not allowed to go to parties or movies or to wear anything other than a dress outside the house. My life consisted of home, school and church. If an event didn't have anything to do with one of those activities, it was taboo. Considering my track record, I'm sure you'll have no trouble believing that our oh-so-sanctimonious preacher tried to put the move on me. Apparently he took the "love one another" doctrine very seriously.

Around 1959 or 1960, my uncle was diagnosed with cancer and was unable to work. We must have been nearly destitute, because the church folks brought us food and the Salvation Army brought me toys and clothes (another brush with haute couture).

In the seventh grade, I was still immature and I acted pretty goofy. One day we held a mock court trial to decide a class issue and the students selected me as one of the "lawyers." Later, the new teacher told me she was surprised that the students selected me, because of how "silly" I was. But she said that when I got into the role of "lawyer," I became serious and competent and she was impressed with me. She went on to advise me to concentrate on my more serious side. And so I did.

I believe that my consciously suppressing that "childish" behavior, attitude and vision negatively influenced my ability to view life from a humorous perspective. And I have often taken life and myself way too seriously since then. What my seventh-grade teacher did not understand was that I was using humor as a shield from the traumas of my childhood. I *needed* some humor in my life! I also did not want to see anyone else unhappy, so my "clown" emerged. If one of my schoolmates was feeling down or had a problem, the clown would try desperately to cheer them up with her antics. I really needed the ability to see the humorous side of life, but my teacher managed to squelch even that little pleasure. Luckily, my silly clown emerged again later and I put her to good use!

In high school, I had only a few close friends, because making friends was difficult for me. When my best girlfriend married at 16, I cried for days. (I did eventually make several other friends, thank you.) I only had three or four dates in those years because I was ashamed of the house I lived in, the clothes I wore, and the people I lived with. My aunt and uncle both used snuff and kept spit cans by their chairs in front of the TV where they sat to watch wrestling. At night, when I went into the kitchen and turned on the lights, what seemed like 8,000 roaches would scurry all over the place. Not exactly a showplace of culture to entertain dates or friends. After high school, I couldn't wait to get away from that "awful" place and my aunt's strict eye.

The Great Escape

One day my aunt and uncle went to buy groceries and I left. A schoolmate and I rented a furnished apartment and moved in together. My aunt was furious and refused to speak to me for years after that. Much to my dismay, however, I escaped from the hated sun porch and fell into reality. I had no car and didn't even know how to drive. I couldn't cook, but I did know how to clean house, because everywhere I had lived, they made sure I did that. I had a job as a file clerk with Georgia Power, and I knew to always pay my bills on time. I'm happy to say that I have never had bad credit.

I began to explore the activities I was never allowed to do while living with my aunt and uncle. I went to night clubs, drank alcohol, danced, blew off church, had friends over, dated some, and wore jeans (gasp!) out on the street. What a rebel! My job paid well enough for me to keep money in my pocket. I loved being independent and having friends around. Of course, I was still immature, insecure and extremely sensitive. I had a lot of growing up left to do.

After a year or so, my roommate fell in love and I had to move again. So I rented a new apartment, bought some furniture, and began living alone. It was difficult, because the pocket money I always used to have was no longer available. Now I only had enough money left to pay my bills. I couldn't afford a car, so I rode the bus back and forth to work. I had to walk about ten blocks to a grocery store and lugging the packages home was a real struggle.

Even worse than having no money was being alone. Sometimes at night, the loneliness was unbearable. I couldn't call any member of my family. My aunt wasn't speaking to me, my mother lived in Virginia, my two brothers had lives of their own. One or the other of them was frequently in jail for some offense, and later they were both in the military. Of course, none of us were close, because we had not lived together in years. I did have a friend who was great about taking me places and talking, but of course, he had a life of his own, too. So my support system was nonexistent.

After a while, however, I began making some friends at work. In fact, two girlfriends asked me to move to Hawaii with them. I resisted at first, but then decided to go for it—another great escape. I had $200 to my name.

15

The second night we were there, we met some Army boys who were headed for Viet Nam. I immediately fell in love with one of them and eventually came to worship him. He wasn't particularly interested in me, but I was determined.

My friends and I soon got jobs; I was selling cemetery plots and urns door-to-door to people who didn't speak English (I didn't speak Chinese or Hawaiian). Our office was actually in the cemetery! Selling was not my forte and I don't think I ever sold a single urn. I also tried selling magazine subscriptions by phone, but that wasn't much more successful than selling cemetery plots!

Later I answered the phone and did light clerical work for a little company that upholstered restaurant booths. The office was filthy, and so were the owner and all the men who worked there. I'm not sure they ever bathed, their hair was never combed, their clothes were dirty, and they always had grime under their fingernails. They were dirty, but I was ignorant. One day I had to write a check for the company and I asked the owner if I was supposed to sign it. The men laughed so hard that I wanted to climb under one of the booths. I'm not even sure how I survived in Hawaii at first.

Eventually one of the girls married a Navy man, my other roommate changed jobs and moved out, and I was stranded alone. By this time, I worked as a secretary to a man who shipped meat. It paid almost nothing, so I was in a nowhere job with no money and no friends…again. Finally I borrowed money from two neighbors in my apartment complex and returned home to Atlanta. Yes, I paid all the money back.

After returning from Hawaii, I got the file clerk job back at Georgia Power. Later, I got a job in a secretarial pool with a different company. The only typing I had done was in high school typing classes. I panicked when I sat down at the electric typewriter. When a position opened up as secretary for a vice president, I applied and got it. What a shock! I didn't know shorthand (I later took a correspondence course), and had only learned to operate an electric typewriter down in the secretarial pool. I began to think seriously about going back to school, but thought I was too stupid to pass the entrance exam or do the work.

I stayed in touch with the boy I had met in Hawaii and chased

16

him unmercifully. He came to visit me a couple of times and decided to stay in Atlanta. We eventually married.

I never had any doubts about marrying him. He was the first man who had ever treated me with kindness and respect, and it was intoxicating. He had goals, ambition and business savvy. I thought the sun rose and set on him. In fact, it wasn't until many years later that I realized that the day our wedding rings arrived at the store, he never even bothered to pick them up. He told me the wrong rings had been sent. This man not only did not want to get married, he didn't love me. I had made the decision, subconsciously, to ignore all the red flags.

The company I worked for was sold and my husband wanted me to work as a waitress in the high-end restaurant where he worked. He taught me to be an ACE waitress so we could get lost of tips (OK, maybe it was the miniskirt I wore). I had never dealt with the public or been a waitress, and wow, did I ever get an education! But I liked the work and meeting the people. The hard part was men running their hands up my leg if I stepped too close to the table and people who put me down just because I was a waitress. That's the way they made themselves feel important. But my husband's dream was to own a restaurant, and this is how people learn the business. We slaved away, took extra jobs whenever we could, and saved every penny.

Eventually we met a man who had the money we needed. My husband had the expertise and I had the elbow grease, so we opened our first restaurant. I worked right along beside him: I cleaned the public restrooms before breakfast every morning, helped keep the books (scary), and was hostess, bus person, cashier and server. Right from the beginning, the restaurant was a huge success.

We were doing well. But even though I encouraged him from the start and worked hard to build the business, I was never made a partner nor did I ever have any "legal" claim to the business. What's wrong with that picture?

In time, we opened more restaurants. Maybe you've heard of them: Provino's and Scalini's Italian restaurants in Atlanta. Yes, I am the original "eggplant parmigiana mom." You can read about it in an article entitled "Rush Delivery" in People magazine, October 21, 2002, Page 126.

This is John Bogino, Bob Bogino and me "recreating" the picture from People magazine that goes along with the story about the eggplant parmigiana urban legend (taken June 2005). The legend is that if you are expecting a baby and you're overdue, if you go to Scalini's on Cobb Parkway and eat the eggplant parmigiana, you will deliver in the morning.

All of the restaurants did well. They provided a good life for us—a life of financial and material success I would never have known otherwise. We had some good times and great laughs. Soon I became pregnant. We had made enough money to finally move from an apartment into a house and we hired a housekeeper. I was happy— until we brought our first child home from the hospital. I had no idea what to do, and although it kills me to admit it, I came close to abusing her. Thank heavens I consciously decided that I didn't want to treat my child like I had been treated. I didn't want to be like the people who had raised me. I didn't realize it at the time, but that was a very important decision. I went out and found some help on how to raise children and I read whatever I could on the subject. I was by no means a perfect mother, but it could have been a lot worse without that decision. I was much better at coping with motherhood by the time my son was born four years later.

Our marriage soon became stifling and repressive. My husband's idea of parenting was that a mother didn't have many activities besides home and hearth. He never changed a diaper, never bought a birthday present, not even for me. He also had a few other "interests," but I looked the other way. I was always too afraid to speak up for fear he would divorce me. I thought I just had to learn to live with whatever came my way. I felt powerless and had no self-respect. I thought I had no right to assert myself, indulge in activities, or pursue any dreams I might have. Heck, I didn't even know I was allowed to HAVE dreams!

That's what childhood abuse does to a person. It tricks your psyche into believing that you are of no consequence. It makes you play the victim role throughout your life, and it can be passed on to succeeding generations. My mother, her sister and her brother had an unstable childhood too. Their mother, my biological grandmother, was an alcoholic and loved to party (at least I know I come by my love of a good party honestly). At any rate, my grandfather wanted out of the marriage and they divorced. My mother and my aunt went with their dad, and my uncle, being the youngest, stayed with their mother. Within two years, however, he wound up in a foster home. The story goes that my mother and aunt went to an orphanage. My father did live with his parents when he was a child, but his father beat him, and he, in turn, according to my brother, beat his sons (my

19

brothers). I believe that both my parents fell into the quagmire of victim thinking. This behavior led to my mother's leaving herself open for abuse, being sent to prison, and denying her talents and dreams. It led to my father's suffering an early death. I believe this is where my surviving brother, the one with the website, operates from. He has never been able to "shake off" the past. He can't forgive my mother nor forget the abuse he suffered from our father and others. This inability to get past victim thinking has negatively affected his ability to be successful in life. He really is quite brilliant, as was our mother, but he hides that brilliance under the shroud of martyrdom he pulls over his shoulders.

To illustrate my point, here are some startling statistics from http://www.prevent-abuse-now.com/stats.htm:

"Approximately 95% of teenage prostitutes have been sexually abused." (Source: CCPCA, 1992)

"Approximately 31% of women in prison state that they had been abused as children." (Source: United States Department of Justice, 1991)

"Previous research established evidence for a cycle of violence: People who were abused and neglected in childhood are more likely than those who were not to become involved in criminal behavior, including violent crime, later in life." (Source: Victims of Childhood Sexual Abuse—Later Criminal Consequences by Cathy Spatz Widom, *NIJ Research in Brief,* March 1995)

Victim thinking can be dangerous on many levels, but you don't have to wallow in that mire or stay in the role of victim—the choice is yours. Make the right one.

The Metamorphosis

Shortly after our daughter was born, I began to wonder why I felt so bad, why I was always depressed, why I was angry most of the time, why I didn't like myself, and why I thought I was useless. I began to think, "Surely life isn't meant to be like this," and decided to find out how life could be better for me. The decision I had made earlier that I didn't want to be like the people who had raised me was proving to be a blessing in my life. I genuinely wanted to be respected and to treat others with respect. I was better at respecting others than myself, but this focus was still an important factor in keeping me on a positive track.

It wasn't easy to learn to respect myself. I had no skills and no self-esteem. I felt that I had never accomplished anything and that I was worthless. I even thought everyone else felt that way—that these feelings were normal. Finally I made the decision to begin mental healing through therapy. Talk about painful! It was during this time, however, that I learned how those other people's decisions had affected my life. And I began to understand that I had the power to think and feel differently about myself. Those other people were the screw-ups, not me. In fact, I remember telling my therapist that I polished my husband's shoes. He asked, "You don't lick them, do you?" From then on, John had to polish his own shoes and I began the long night's journey into day.

My therapist and I soon decided that I should develop a plan to assert myself. What I am about to tell you may seem trivial, but it became a catalyst for the actions I took to pull myself up by the bootstraps.

My husband was adamant that we were not going to use any credit cards and would pay cash for everything. I thought it would be a good idea to have one or two cards: one for gas, because I never seemed to have any cash, and maybe one for shopping. My doctor agreed that getting a credit card seemed reasonable and advised me to do it. It would be one small step in asserting myself. So one day, I went into a major department store, determined to fulfill my mission and open a charge account. I began walking toward the escalator, but I stopped, turned around, and headed out of the store. I told myself, "If I do this, he will divorce me. I shouldn't rock the boat. I have no right to defy my husband." I already had a dozen excuses to tell my therapist. But I heard a voice inside my head: "Diane, if you don't do this now, you'll never do it." I listened. I turned around, went up the escalator and opened an account. That small decision was the first step on the road to discovering who I was and, more importantly, who I wanted to become.

It takes but one positive thought when given a chance to survive and thrive to overpower an entire army of negative thoughts.
~~Robert H. Schuller (1926)
Ordained minister

Sometimes what we think is the most worthless of talents can catapult us into a better, more fulfilled life. In addition to my Little Miss Muffet performance in grade school, I was president of the Drama Club in high school and acted in several plays. As an adult, I got interested in magic and became a magic clown. Remember, I said you would see the little clown reemerge. In that persona, I was finally granted permission to be silly, outrageous and totally off the wall. I performed at kid's birthday parties and fought with a chicken. (You had to be there.) Not one of the children ever said, "Stop being so silly!" And my peers selected me Magician of the Year for Greater Atlanta.

I went on to perform in several commercials, some plays, and a movie. Hey, I got my name in the credits and they even spelled it right! The name of the movie was "Something Special." (No offense to Patty Duke, but it wasn't special at all.) I also emceed shows at my children's school and tried my hand at comedy.

Then I did some modeling, both print and runway. At 5'6", I was not really tall enough, but I persisted and was finally hired by a top department store as a runway model. One day I was modeling a black satin dress with rhinestone straps. A gentleman in the audience said to me, "You really look good in that dress." Wow! Someone thought I looked good. I couldn't believe it! And, of course, I bought the dress immediately after the show.

That brief stint in show business helped me feel better about my looks and I began to gain even more confidence. It also helped me realize that

I didn't want to lead a shallow life. Then my husband, who didn't want any part of a wife who had self-confidence, a career, and a mind of her own, came to me and said, "It's either our marriage or your job."

> I was shaking in my shoes, but I managed to work up the couage to whisper, "I have to work."
> He asked, "Whether you're married or not?"
> I answered, "Whether I'm married or not."

Well, the divorce didn't come, at least not then. I later discovered a couple more of his other "agendas," but he promised to put them aside. We tried to make a go of our relationship, but it wasn't very long before he felt the need to pursue his other "pastimes" again and the end finally came.

Ending our 20-year marriage devastated me to the point that I was unable to function, but I knew I had to get unstuck. So one afternoon, I wrote down: "Take the dog to the vet." That was my assignment for the next day. It was the only thing I had to do; it was the only thing I could *manage* to do. Once I accomplished that chore, I began doing more and more. But soon I was faced with something that had never even entered my mind.

My days as a magician!

The metamorphosis

My runway modeling days

My husband, Jerry
Simmons, and me

My grandson,
Nathan

I woke up one morning with the realization that everything we owned was in John's name: the businesses I had helped build, the house I lived in, the car I was driving. I had no education, no permanent job and two children to feed and raise. No scary movie I know can top that! I was in a panic because I had no idea how I was going to survive. One day I thought I would poison the cat and dog, shoot my two children, and then kill myself. Thank goodness that plan didn't come together! That brings us to where we began— my clinging to the kitchen counter with white knuckles and aching fingers.

My children and I were provided for in the divorce agreement, but I soon realized that I needed to get a job. (You can't fool *me* for very long!) My work history was varied. In addition to my jobs as file clerk, secretary, unsuccessful telemarketer and showbiz wannabe, I had only worked in our restaurants. What was I going to do?

A "showbiz" friend eventually got me involved with a public relations firm that was developing a training program to teach executives how to interview with TV, press and radio reporters. They wanted me to be the trainer. Me? Are you kidding? But I took the job, worked on commission, and was still pretty much "starving."

In one of my first training classes, a male doctor stood up to his full 6'4" height and yelled at me, "Why the hell are we doing this?" I could only stand there frozen. Fortunately, one of the female doctors reminded him of the reasons and he settled down. I was definitely having second thoughts about going into training! Soon after that, I opened my own résumé business and lost about $20,000. (I hate it when that happens.)

During this career-seeking time, I married again. Another mistake. My second husband had problems with anger and was abusive to his own son. I was attracted to him because he had a college education, came from a good family and, well, hey, he was interested in me!

The résumé business and the marriage both lasted about six months. My daughter was so angry with me for marrying this jerk that she ran away from home, dropped out of school, became pregnant and got married. She was 15. Today my grandson is 15, going on 30, and just beautiful (I can send more pictures if you like).

25

But I digress. After the "owning my own business" fiasco, I got a job as an administrative assistant in an aerospace recruiting firm, but the jerks fired me! Next came a job in a hotel's human resources department for $8 an hour. I barely survived; I had to take money out of my savings every other month or so just to make ends meet. My son and I sold our jewelry, computers and any other items we could do without just so we could have some cash. At one point, I was working full-time, my son was on three (count 'em, three) basketball teams, and I going to college at night.

Yes, I took the giant risk of applying to a college. When I got the results of my entrance exams, I noticed the words "Honor Student." I put the envelope down and thought, "Good grief, these idiots have gotten my records mixed up with somebody else's!" As it turned out, neither the college nor I was quite the idiot I thought.

I studied human resources, but I had always known that I loved to teach, so I pursued a career as a trainer with the hotel chain and continued to work on getting my life into perspective. I did well in school, but I only finished about three years.

I hadn't gone to college sooner because I believed I just wasn't smart enough. But according to *Straight Thinking, Common Sense, and Good Arguments* (http://mentalhelp.net/psychelp/chap14/), "…straight thinking and reasoning skills aren't just inherited; accurate thinking is the result of inherited ability *and* a lot of experience and wisdom…. A true 'expert' needs enormous stored knowledge (10+ years of intense study and practice), a mind capable of systematically searching that memory for useful information, and the skill to detect defective, distorted thinking. Being smart isn't just a matter of being born that way."

So you must begin today—now—to get your "smarts" through the trial and error of time and experience. How can you quickly acquire this "stored knowledge, experience and wisdom"?

First, don't be bamboozled by the word "wisdom." You don't have to have a long gray beard, bushy eyebrows and a humpback in order to have wisdom. A good definition is: "[The] ability to apply knowledge or experience or understanding or common sense and insight" (http://www.thefreedictionary.com/wisdom). Knowledge can be gained through any number of avenues. If you're a young person, regardless of whether you're in high school or college, stay in school.

That is your job until you graduate.

If you're older—you know, with the gray beard, bushy eyebrows and humpback—you can still enroll in school. Trust me, they will take your money! After all, you are going to be 40, 50, 60, 70 or 80 anyway, and going to school will keep you active, sharp and out of your kids' hair. You may have knowledge and experience that you don't even realize. Answer these few questions and see for yourself. Your first thoughts are usually the best. When you're finished, go back over what you've written and look for patterns of knowledge, experience and wisdom.

(1) Think back to the age of 6 or 7. What did you love to pretend being?

_____

_____

(2) As a teenager, what did you enjoy doing?

_____

_____

(3) What hobbies do you have? List anything you enjoy doing that you don't have to be motivated to do—something you simply love doing. It can be a full-fledged hobby like collecting trains to a pastime like simply watching movies.

_____

_____

(4) Think about any volunteer work you you've done. List the organization, what you did and why you did it.

Organization: _____

Your role: _____

Why did you volunteer?_____

_____

_____

Organization:_____

Your role:_____

Why did you volunteer?_____

_____

_____

Organization:_____

Your role:_____

Why did you volunteer?_____

_____

_____

(5) Think of three people you know and the jobs they perform. These should not be people who are doing the exact job you are doing. List three things about *their* jobs that you like and three things you dislike.

1st Person:_____

Job:_____

Likes	Dislikes

2nd Person:_____

Job:_____

Likes	Dislikes

3rd Person: _____

Job: _____

Likes	Dislikes

(6) List three jobs you've had. List three things you liked or disliked about each.

1st Job:

Likes	Dislikes

2nd Job

Likes	Dislikes

3rd Job:

Likes	Dislikes

(7) List three areas in life where you feel you've made a difference, either for a person or a situation.

1._____

2._____

3._____

(8) List three times you felt strongly about something and stood up for that belief.

1._____

2._____

3._____

(9) Name three of the most exciting things you've ever done.

1._____

2._____

3._____

(10) List three of your proudest accomplishments.

1._____

2._____

3._____

Now go back over these lists and write down patterns you see from what you have written.

Things/Tasks I've Enjoyed doing	Things I Value	Things I Dislike

You now have a list of your own wisdom, knowledge and experience, as well as your likes and dislikes. This information will arm you to make better decisions about your life from now on. Use it wisely, unlike me and my next bad choice. Yes, another guy. For this one, I subleased my house, moved out of state, and purchased a house with him. Like other men in my life, he was verbally abusive, and eventually he became physically abusive. The important thing is that I got out right away and once again I left town with no job, no money, and no place to stay. I finally found a hotel that had far less than a five-star rating. The rug was so dirty that I couldn't walk on it in bare feet, and I woke up with a roach in my bed one morning. I tried to find a job, but didn't have much luck. Finally my daughter talked her father into lending me the money to move back to Atlanta, and I escaped again. (Yes, I paid back every nickel.)

As you can see, most of the decisions I made in my early life weren't the best. But no one is *born* knowing how to make good decisions. Good decisions come from practice. When you don't have people who care about you teaching you what is and is not a good choice, it colors every decision you make.

My life changed because I learned and used the 11 skills and attributes outlined in this book. They will also help you reach your goals, I promise. Along with my own comments, I've included some quotes to help keep you

31

motivated. Make copies of the most meaningful ones for you and put them where you will see them every day.

Disclaimer: Make no mistake, I've had years of therapy. If you have deep-seated emotional problems, I urge you to find a good therapist. Getting psychiatric or psychological help doesn't carry the stigma it once did. If money is a concern, your company may have an Employee Assistance Program available to you. You may even find someone to work with through your state or county.

If you have the funds, you might consider hiring a life coach. Just remember that a life coach is not typically trained to deal with serious emotional or mental disorders. A good coach, however, can be a catalyst to help you get back on track, develop self-esteem and reach your dreams.

Step 1: Get to Know Yourself— How Turtles Hurdle Hurdles

Turtles are known to be slow-moving. I was slow-developing. No, my mother didn't carry me for 18 months. Yes, I am physically OK. (Well, a few areas could stand improvement, but that's a whole different book.) My mental state is stable (well...). I'm talking about my socio-emotional state now. As I said earlier, I have hidden in a shell most of my life. I probably had all of four dates during my high school years, I didn't get my driver's license until the age of 25, I had no idea what career I wanted to pursue until my 30s, I didn't begin college until my early 40s, and I didn't find the love of my life until my 50s. Like I said, the slow-moving turtle has nothing on me!

And talk about hurdles! I have allowed emotion, people and experiences to slow my journey. I still regret that I didn't "have my act together" earlier in life. It has taken me 50 years to get to this point because I didn't take the time to get to know myself. Many people don't enjoy being alone, but I believe everyone needs quiet time to just be with themselves. In other words, turn down the volume of all the things that are distracting you. This time is perfect for putting your life into perspective, getting to know who you are, and discovering your true (and honest) values. You can't really get your life together until you establish a values system for yourself. The exercise you took in the previous chapter will help you begin to know who you are and to determine your own value system.

He who knows others is learned. He who knows himself is wise.

~~Lao Tse (604 BC)
Chinese philosopher

Often, people who have not been taught values grow up not being clear about right and wrong, good and bad, or even what is and isn't right for them. In other words, it's not only a question of morals, but which behaviors are self-benefiting and which are self-defeating. Too often, abuse victims choose defeating behaviors because that's what they know. It sounds sick, but those are the behaviors they feel comfortable with. I wore that "comfortable" armor for many years. I had no idea what I valued in life, and I certainly had no idea what I praised about myself. Because of that, I had no clue about how or where to begin designing a life. It is fitting that I called that behavior "armor." It doesn't let you out to explore your good, your not-so-good, your potential, your intelligence or your beauty. It also keeps out those who could love, appreciate and help you.

Your own armor is always the toughest to break through. It's easy to throw rocks at someone else's armor or to help them break off a piece, but we may even be *protective* of our own armor, kidding ourselves into thinking that we need it to survive.

So to begin breaking up your armor from the inside out, get rid of the idea that you need that deceptive defense. Those so-called "needs" are only crutches. If you use the crutches, they only serve to cripple you emotionally. So here's what I want you to do: Take some 3x5 cards and write down the things that have formed your armor.

Example:
>FEAR (False Evidence Appearing Real)

(List three fears and ask yourself, "Are these fears realistic?" If any *are* real, think of ways to dissolve those fears.)

1. _____
2. _____
3. _____

LACK OF SKILLS

Write down, "I know I have many skills that are useful to me and others."

(Then list a few of your useful skills. If you can't list any, think of ways to attain these skills if you need them to realize your goals.)

Whatever items have become molded around your psyche and are holding you back, make a card for each of them and write a positive affirmation on it. Make the affirmation something meaningful to you, for example:

If you have health issues: "I am healthier each day because I take better care of myself every day. I deserve proper care and am worth the time I spend on my good health."

If you have money management issues: "More money is coming into my life. I manage my money well. I use my money for the good of myself and others."

If you have love issues: "I am attracting the kind of person I want in my life. I deserve to be loved and cared for. I am lovable."

There are more affirmations on pages 48-49, and here are some hints for writing your own:
1. Write in the present tense.
2. Keep the affirmations positive.
3. Read your affirmation(s) every day and back them up with feelings.
4. Write them several times.

Read these cards for 21 days first thing every morning and once every evening before you drift off to sleep. You will see your armor begin to crack and chip. Soon it will fall into a million little pieces.

You gain strength, courage and confidence by every experience in which you really stop to look fear in the face. You must do the thing which you think you cannot do.

~~Eleanor Roosevelt (1884-1962)
American diplomat, writer, 32nd First Lady

Being able to look inward and examine yourself—to understand what you value and who you are—is the first step toward a successful and happy life. People who are unable to be alone with themselves never become acquainted with their own best friend. People who run from conflict and confrontation never know what they stand for or how much they can bear. Those who don't know their strengths and weaknesses never know who or what they need to incorporate or leave out of their lives to reach success.

I believe that one reason people refuse to look at themselves is that they think it's the *other person* who needs to change. The truth is that both people in any type of harmful relationship probably need to change. Every relationship—whether intimate, work or play—has two sides. Each side brings the good, the bad and the ugly into the relationship.

As Glenna Salsbury writes in her book, *The Art of the Fresh Start*, "In every difficult decision, your mind and emotions are really considering only three options." She goes on to say that these three options are to alter the situation, avoid the situation, or accept the situation. It's a little difficult to avoid yourself, so your best choice is to accept yourself. At this point, whatever needs to be altered can be addressed. As far as difficult relationships, however, your optimum choice is to avoid them as much as possible. Still, you're always going to experience some conflict with others, so you need the "emotional muscle" to get through them. This book will help you develop that muscle. Just remember that difficult *intimate* relationships are always to be avoided. If they can't be altered, you *must not* accept them. You deserve and need better.

Another reason people fail to look inside is because self-examination can sometimes go at a turtle's pace, which exaggerates the pain.

But the work is critical. If you don't know what you value, it will be very difficult, if not impossible, to reach a clear decision on the direction you want your life to take.

When learning what you value, remember to include yourself. You have to accept yourself as worthy of nourishment, care and love. You must also decide that you are worthy of development—physically, mentally and emotionally.

A true knowledge of ourselves is knowledge of our power.

~~Mark Rutherford (aka William Hale White) (1831-1913), Victorian author

---

One way to understand what you value is to think about what you would tell someone who asked, "What do you think is most important in life?" How would you answer them? Imagine that this person is your child, godchild, grandchild, great grandchild, someone you are mentoring, or someone who is attempting to establish their own values. When you're sure of your values, your goals become easier to reach, because your values form the hull of the ship that will carry you to your destination and keep your ship afloat in the stormy seas of doubt and fear.

It may help to think of your values as tools to help you get through life. One of my values is honesty, and I have always been grateful for the decision I made to be completely honest. I've not enjoyed a perfect record, but that decision has served me well in both personal and working relationships. It has helped me make better decisions and it has enhanced my personal reputation. Living an honest life brings me back to a value that gives me direction. Being honest would not allow me to stray to any lifestyle that involved being unscrupulous.

Here's the real beauty of what I'm telling you. The ability to choose is one of the most powerful tools you have. I had a client who was (and still is) very religious. She kept saying that she was waiting for God to tell her what he wanted her to do with her life. But the book of *Genesis* says that when God created Adam, he gave Adam the gift of choice. Adam was allowed to choose whatever name he wanted for the animals, he chose to have a mate, and he was allowed to choose whether or not to accept Eve.

If you're of a more political mind, this country and our society are all about having the right to make choices for ourselves. Lands across the world are stained with the blood of those who have fought and died for this great privilege of ours. America does not hold anyone hostage; the people here *choose* to be here. (Now that I've gotten *that* off my chest....) The power of choice has never been taken from us, at least not by God or any universal power we might believe in, or by any other country. If we lose that power, we take it from ourselves—we steal our own birthright.

In my own life, honesty has helped me to attract people and opportunities that would not have presented themselves had I made the choice to be dishonest. Yes, it's just that simple. Having honesty as a value also means you will be truthful with yourself about the best life for you—not your friend's or family's idea of what's right for you.

Anytime we need to perform a task, we need the proper knowledge, tools and techniques to accomplish it correctly. You get the knowledge by knowing yourself, the tools are the values you establish for yourself, and the technique is what you develop as you perform the task over and over again.

If you want to be truly successful, invest in yourself to get the knowledge you need to find your unique factor. When you find it and focus on it and persevere, your success will blossom.
~~Sidney Madwed
Professional speaker, consultant, lyricist, author

Because I have learned to value myself, I have also found the love of my life—my current and last husband. He supports me in every effort, is proud of me and my accomplishments, and loves me for who I am. Finding love in your life is another benefit of finding out who you are, because you become the kind of person you want to attract. That person appears in your life as if by magic. The fact that he brings me breakfast in bed every morning ain't too bad either!

Remember, however, that going to the extreme and valuing only your-self can express itself in some very negative ways. I'm speaking here about people who let their egos rule their lives—people who think of no one but themselves. According to http://www. hardylaw.net/mental.html, the definition of "narcissistic disorder" is:

"A pattern of traits and behaviors which signify infatuation and obses-sion with one's self to the exclusion of all others and the egotistic and ruthless pursuit of one's gratification, dominance and ambition.... An all-per-vasive pattern of grandiosity (in fantasy, or behavious [sic]), need for admira-tion or adulation and lack of empathy, usually beginning by early adulthood and present in various contexts. [This disorder] is predominantly a male trait."

Sparing you the psycho mumble jumble, it goes on to say that the disor-der can become evident in acts of self-destruction and the destruction of others. This is not the place to go with ego.

The shadow is a moral problem that challenges the whole ego-personality, for no one can become conscious of the shadow without considerable moral effort. To become conscious of it involves recognizing the dark aspects of the personal-ity as present and real. This act is the essential condition for any kind of self-knowledge and it, therefore, as a rule, meets with considerable re-sistance. Indeed, self-knowledge as a psycho-ther-apeutic measure frequently requires much pains-taking work extending over a long period of time.

~~Carl Jung (1875-1961)
Swiss psychiatrist

In reading the lives of great men, I found that the first victory they won was over them-selves...self-discipline with all of them came first.

~~Harry S. Truman (1884-1953)
33rd US President

Self-awareness is surely critical because some of the major obstacles to clear thinking are within ourselves, i.e., our defenses, our emotions, our blind spots.

~~http://mentalhelp.net/psych

You never conquer a mountain; mountains can't be conquered. You conquer yourself—your hopes, your fears.

~~Jim Whitaker (1929)
Mountaineer, adventurer,
speaker, environmentalist

Step 2: Use Positive Self-Talk—
Whisper Sweet Nothings in Your Own Ear

After you have established your value system, the next area to concentrate on is your self-talk. This step may seem so small that it can be ignored and pushed aside, but it actually serves as the foundation that reaches into the depth of your psyche, emotions and reality. Remember that your subconscious mind has no judgments of its own—it believes whatever messages you send it. It makes no difference whether those messages are good, bad or indifferent. Therefore, it is vitally important that the everyday visions you send are the ones you want to manifest in your life.

We all talk to ourselves. Joe Kolezynski, MBA, MA, states in an article at http://www.selfhelpmagazine.com/articles/sports/selftalk.html, *Belief, Self-Talk, and Performance Enhancement:* "It has been established by psychologists and neuroscientists that every person in the world carries on an ongoing dialog, or self-talk, of between 150 and 300 words a minute. This works out to be between 45,000 and 51,000 thoughts a day."

So if you are going to talk to yourself anyway, why not make your message uplifting and positive? We would never dream of speaking to someone else the way we speak to ourselves. When a child is trying to walk and falls down, we don't belittle him or her— we give encouragement to try again. If someone we know is trying to learn a new skill, we don't hurl negative feedback at them. Instead, we focus on something good the person did and then offer a way to try it differently next time for improvement. Why don't we give ourselves the same respect? Self-respect is an amazing catalyst. Because when you respect yourself, others begin to respect you as well. How do you learn to respect yourself?

Let's go to the movies. Many of you will remember the movie "It's a Good Life" starring Jimmy Stewart. If you're not familiar with it, watch the DVD, and think about your own life. In a nutshell, Stewart, playing George Bailey, found himself in a desperate situation and contemplated suicide. An angel stopped him and took him on a tour through the lives of people he knew. Only on this tour, they had never known Bailey.

Think about the people you have touched. How would their lives be different without you? What about your spouse, sister, brother, parents, friends and business acquaintances? What about your children—why, they wouldn't even *be here* without you!

Let's take a scenario from my own life, and believe me, this isn't something I think about all the time! Because I did something a little wild, and fell in love, a business was created. This business not only provided well for my family, it also supplied hundreds of people with jobs; provided craftsman, vendors and the city with revenue; and gave food and fun times to millions of people. I've never stopped to think about that before, but it makes me feel all warm and fuzzy inside to know that I was involved in making that happen. It's part of my self-respect. Stop now and think about how you can respect yourself by acknowledging the differences you've made in other people's lives.

Person	How I've Made a Positive Difference for them

Use Positive Self-Talk-
Whisper Sweet Nothings in Your Own Ear

Another way to begin building self-respect is to remember that what comes out of our mouth is just a small part of a deeper communication system. The words we hear float up from the foundation that has been built within us over the years. To be successful, you must tear down any negative foundation and build a more positive one. Begin by getting rid of negative thinking...especially about you! You can always work on what needs improvement later, and there will always be plenty of people around who are all too eager to point out your faults—don't you be one of them. Try this exercise for 30 days:

List six of your positive attributes:

(1) _____

(2) _____

(3) _____

(4) _____

(5) _____

(6) _____

Now take each property you've listed and list two positive or productive ways you've used that characteristic to your advantage in the past. Then list at least one way you can use that attribute in the future to reach your goals.

(1) Attribute _____

I used this in the past to accomplish the following:

_____

_____

_____

_____

Use Positive Self-Talk-
Whisper Sweet Nothings in Your Own Ear

I can use this attrtibute in the future to accomplish the following:

_____

_____

_____

_____

(2) Attribute: _____

I used this in the past to accomplish the following:

_____

_____

_____

_____

I can use this attribute in the future to accomplish the following:

_____

_____

_____

_____

(3) Attribute _____

I used this in the past to accomplish the following:

_____

_____

_____

_____

I can use this attribute in the future to accomplish the following:

_____

_____

_____

_____

(4) Attribute _____

I used this in the past to accomplish the following:

_____

_____

_____

_____

I can use this attribute in the future to accomplish the following:

_____

_____

_____

_____

(5) Attribute _____

I used this in he past to accomplish the following:

_____

_____

_____

_____

I can use this attribute in the future to accomplish the following:

_____

_____

_____

_____

(6) Attribute _____

I used this in the past to accomplish the following:

_____

_____

_____

I can use this attribute in the future to accomplish the following:

_____

_____

_____

As you do this exercise each day for the next 30 days, try to come up with as many of your positive attributes as possible. It's OK to occasionally repeat a characteristic. As you rewrite some of them, new ideas will come to you about how you have used that attribute in the past to be successful and you'll think of new ways to use it to accomplish future goals.

The beautiful part about this step is that it costs you nothing, it's something you can do every single day, you can start it any time, you will also learn how to incorporate accountability into other areas of your life (like your self-worth and well-being), and it works miracles for your growth.

This exercise is based on "behavioral interviewing," a type of interviewing that human resource personnel use with job candidates. The reasoning behind this technique suggests that how a person acted or handled a situation in the past is a good indication of how they will act or handle a similar situation in the future. So you will get double your money for this exercise. Not only will you begin to build a more positive foundation for your emotional well-being, but you will be ready for that next all-important interview! What a deal!

Positive self-talk will also help you become your own person. Letting others decide what your life should be like is no life at all. Ask yourself what YOU want. Giving other people power over you and your future is a mistake too often made by those who perceive themselves to be powerless. When you use positive self-talk, the words of someone who is belittling you or trying to bring you down will soon sound so foreign to you that you will dismiss those words as the lies they are.

I'm lumping physical abuse in this category as well. No one has permission to lay their hands on you unless you say it's OK. Remember that people who have to denigrate others in ANY manner are the ones with the issues... not you! These kinds of people are like bats that suck blood. If you allow them to continue, they will suck your spirit, your energy, your health, and maybe even the very life out of you.

No one can make you feel inferior without your consent.
~~Eleanor Roosevelt, ibid.

How do you change your self-talk? You can first try to "sweet talk" yourself into stopping, as though you were mothering a two-year-old who was smacking his younger sibling on the head with the dust pan. When that doesn't work, say, "Stop!" whenever you begin to downgrade yourself, even if you have to say it out loud. Then intentionally change the direction of your self-talk.

Instead of saying, "I just can't do this," say, "How can I find a way to do this?" Instead of saying, "I'm useless," say, "I'm just as good as anyone. I have many talents, and I can make good use of those talents to help myself and others."

Instead of saying, "I'm going nowhere at work," say, "What can I do to change my career path?" or "What new skill can I learn to help me change paths?"

This is also the perfect time to begin giving yourself permission and affirmation to do those things you want and need to do to change your life.

For example:

"I give myself permission to ask for help."

"I deserve to be treated with kindness and respect."

"I have my permission to pursue my dreams."

"I deserve to have a happy life, free from worry."

"I have the power to make my own choices in life."

"I can give myself permission to change my life."

"I have the confidence to achieve my goals."

"I deserve love."

If you worry about maintaining your positive self-talk, just remember that it's accomplished in the same way you learned to walk, talk, say your ABCs, and tie your shoes—by repetition. After a while, you won't even *entertain* any negative thoughts about yourself, and probably not about anyone else either. You'll be too busy reaching for your goals.

You must stop beating yourself down with negative remarks, opinions and critiques. Positive self-talk and thoughts will help you get your bootstraps unknotted so they can be free and ready for you to grab hold and PULL!

Watch your thoughts; they become words. Watch your words; they become actions. Watch your actions; they become habits. Watch your habits; they become character. Watch your character; it becomes your destiny.
~~Frank Outlaw (1948)
Ex con artist

The more man meditates upon good thoughts, the better will be his world and the world at large.
~~Confucius (551-479 BC)
Chinese philosopher

You are the key to your success. Never, never let anyone else bring you down.
~~Me!

Don't ever let anyone steal your dreams, your integrity, your courage or your character.
~~Stewart E. White (1873-1946)
Adventurer, author

We are what we repeatedly do. Excellence, then, is not an act, but a habit.
~~Aristotle (384-322 BCE)
Greek philosopher

Step 3: Get a Support System— No Person Is an Island

It's critical that you have a support system—a group of friends who will back you up and be there for you. If you already have a support "group" of only one or two, you need to branch out and meet other people. Constantly relying on one or two individuals will not give you the rich resources or life you crave.

This has been the most difficult step for me. When I had the epiphany that life had to be better than it was, I still could only move forward in the smallest of steps because I had no support. I was still in an environment where no one cared about my needs. Understandably, people who are not sure of themselves, or who have been victimized, find it difficult to interact with others. Even today, it causes me some level of trauma to meet someone for lunch; I don't have the social skills I need to function in such situations. Having been isolated for so long, and having been taught that I was of no consequence or value, I never intentionally put myself in a situation where I could be rejected. I wasn't exposed to social events such as birthday parties, skating outings, camping, girl/boy scouts and the like. Abuse victims feel "different" from everyone else—like we don't fit in. We are always on the peripheral of social interaction. I urge you to get over it. Just take the first small step toward freedom, and then another, and then keep on taking them. Soon your steps will become strides.

Here are some ideas on how to find people who can become a part of your support group:

Meet new people. Begin by placing yourself in a nonthreatening area. I accomplished this by joining associations. At first, I was "just there." I would scurry in and out, hoping that no one would notice me. Later, people began asking me to help with the meetings. Maybe it was just distributing handouts or some other small chore. As I became better known within the group, always being careful to do whatever I said I would do, people began to seek me out for larger tasks like introducing someone, or even managing some small event. Soon I began to volunteer! This is not something I would have readily done in years past. Why? Because I was afraid of being rejected. I mean, come on, who would reject a volunteer? But such is the psyche of a victim.

As I became better known, people began to collaborate with me. Now I am a member of a great "mastermind" group. We meet once a month and share ideas on our respective businesses. The members don't even have to be in the same business—they just have to agree to be supportive of one another, offer encouragement and give gentle critiques. This was a major step for me, but it's just the kind of support system you might need. A mastermind group doesn't have to be for business purposes either; you can form a personal mastermind group. Just be sure that each member of the group is as committed and dedicated as you are to changing their lives.

If the cost of joining an association holds you back, find at least one person you can trust and form a bond with him or her. Then begin to add more people to your group. If your support buddies want to hold "formal" meetings on a regular basis, better yet. Finding supportive people doesn't have to cost you anything but some time. Your group doesn't have to come with the answer to world peace, just the solution to one issue that is defeating someone's success.

According to http://mentalhelp.net/psyhelp/chap14/chap14s.htm, "You must keep in mind that straight thinking requires more than mental rumination by yourself. Ideas must be tested in reality. Talk to others with different views (not just supportive friends). Try out your ideas, see if they work, see if others agree, and see if your ideas can be improved." Two heads, or more, are much better than one.

Other support systems could include family or friends, or the person next door, or someone you meet at school or the PTA. Of course, steer clear of anyone who was abusive to you in the past, including family members. No law says that, just because these people are your family, you must put yourself in their presence.

Hire a coach. Since I'm a life coach, this may sound a little self-promoting, and I apologize for that. But a coach can be an ideal partner for helping you stay on track. A good coach is nonjudgmental, will offer you encouragement and support, and can direct you to appropriate resources so you can learn what you need to know to help yourself and become self-sufficient. A coach is a cross between your therapist and your best friend. What could be better than that?

Learn to network. For years I couldn't do this. It was like jumping in the deep end of the pool with no life jacket. I didn't know what to say or do at networking events and avoided them like the plague. But as I became more comfortable in other social situations, I learned how to network, and I've met some wonderful people. Some of them have become friends; others are just great resources. I can call or email both groups with questions or run ideas past them. The truth is that people like to help people. In one association, our members fall all over each other to help another member. My affiliation with these people has given me many insights, educated me, and saved me many hours of trying to find out things for myself. As an added bonus, this association and the people in it make me feel warm, wonderful, needed and valued.

Networking is also important when looking for that next job. You know, the one you want but think you're unqualified to fill? I give each of my clients a networking booklet to help them realize that they do have resources. They are required to contact each of the people they log in their networking booklet. Here is an abbreviated version for you:

Get a Support System-
No Person Is an Island

Category	Name	Contact Info	Result of Contact
Leads Groups			
Neighbors			
Networing Groups			
Organizations (Political)			
Organizations (Religious)			

Parents of Children's Friends			
Place I Shop			
Relatives			
School Mates			
Service Contacts			

Sports/Social Contacts			
Volunteer Activities			
Other			

Adapted from Michael Farr's job networking model from his company, JIST.

Motivation is what gets you started. Habit is what keeps you going.

~~Jim Rohn
American speaker, author

Not every category will apply to you, but some of them may jog your memory and help you think of someone else. If so, just put it in the "Other" category.

The idea here is to ask your contacts if they know of, or have, whatever it is you need to complete your goals. If they say No, ask if they know of anyone who might. When you call *that* person, you do the same routine. Eventually you will find the individual who has what you need, whether it's training, knowledge or just plain know-how.

Choose dependable friends. The type of people you surround yourself with is extremely important. Avoid people who have bad habits, language or thoughts, or who pull you down in any way. There are plenty of others out there who will find you fascinating and want to be with you, work with you, and soak up your wisdom.

Life is difficult enough; don't go through it alone. Other people become *particularly* important when you are trying to set and accomplish goals, because you need the wisdom of those who have "been there, done that."

Step 4: Find Your Passion—
Do What You Love

What is your purpose in life? What excites you? What could you spend hours on that seem like only minutes? Have you made decisions in your life that have prevented you from pursuing that passion?

In my career-coaching business, I meet many people who are going back and forth to work on automatic pilot. I have clients of all ages who dread going to work, who are miserable while they're at the office, and who probably make everyone around them unhappy as well. They can't wait until the "bell rings" so they can leave.

Many people are employed by companies whose products/services they don't care about, working for people who bring them down, and performing tasks that are meaningless to them. A study by The Conference Board (an independent membership organization for the public interest) shows that nearly 50% of Americans don't like their jobs. How do people wind up like this? Why do we spend so much of our work lives in misery?

Sometimes people just "fall" into professions. For example, I know an individual who handles the payroll in an accounting office. Is that her dream job? No, she wants to be an interior decorator. (And she has the best-looking office in the company!) She got into accounting right out of high school by taking the first job she was offered, and her career progressed from there.

Sometimes folks get stuck in the wrong job because they need money to survive, because they don't like change, because they don't want to spend time and energy just to upset the status quo, or because they're afraid to risk losing even the slightest amount of income. Wake up, people! Do what you love and the money will follow.

The purpose of life, after all, is to live it, to taste experience to the utmost, to reach out eagerly and without fear for newer and richer experience.
~~Eleanor Roosevelt, ibid.

One way I begin to realize what my clients really want to do in life is by just listening to them. The minute they begin to talk about their passion, their whole persona changes. Their eyes light up, a smile appears where there had been none, their entire body responds to this wonderful stimulus, and they can suddenly talk for hours! Pay attention to *yourself* when you talk about different topics, or when you browse in a bookstore, or when a talk show catches your interest, and you will see what I mean. You hang around longer when the topic intrigues you.

What can you do if you're in a job and can't afford to leave and follow your passion? Even getting a little taste of the things you love into your life will help change your outlook. Begin slowly—bring your passion into your hobbies if you can't afford to fully jump in. Attend events in the "arena" you are interested in. Build up contacts, gather information, and always be on the lookout for possible opportunities to do what you love—as a volunteer, or part-time, or in a one-time paid event.

If you are unsure about what you want to do, there are plenty of assessments you can take. These can be obtained from school counselors, from career coaches, or from any number of books on the market. Some of the assessments I offer and the information gained include:
Successful Career Planning
Personal Characteristics
Personal Strengths
Your Basic Needs
Your Present Wants
Your Ideal Environment
Job Indicator (what kind of job you are best suited for)

61

Books to Consider:

Follow Your Dreams by D. Conway Stone (Passages
    Publishing, 1995)

Get Ahead! Stay Ahead! by Dianna Booher (Dianna Booher,
    1997)

*I Could Do Anything If I Only Knew What It Was: How to
    Discover What You Really Want and How to Get It*
    by Barbara Sher (Delacorte Press, 1994)

*I Don't Know What I Want, But I Know It's Not This: A
    Step-by-Step Guide to Finding Gratifying Work*
    by Julie Jansen (Penguin Books, 2003)

Self Matters: Creating Your Life From the Inside Out
    by Phillip C. McGraw, Ph.D. (Simon & Schuster
    Source, 2001)

What Color Is Your Parachute? by Richard Nelson Bolles
    (Ten Speed Press, 2003)

A more inexpensive way is simply to think back to your childhood. What did you pretend to be? Were you an airline pilot? An FBI agent? A doctor? Nurse? Teacher? Astronaut? Housewife? Secretary? CEO? Firefighter? Mom or dad? Storekeeper? What did you daydream about when you were alone and free to concentrate on your favorite thoughts? What excited you about those thoughts? What made you feel whole or real or satisfied with yourself?

Nothing is as real as a dream. The world can change around you, but your dream will not. Responsibilities need not erase it. Duties need not obscure it. Because the dream is within you, no one can take it away.

~~Tom Clancy (1947)
American author

You can escape to that place again. Find some quiet time and an area where you won't be disturbed and just let your mind take its own course. Take a blank sheet of paper or journal with you and be prepared to write down thoughts and ideas to go over later. Don't edit—it just confuses the process and the spontaneity!

Of course your "playtime pretend" list is probably endless, so begin with the ideas that still occur to you most often or your strongest memories. Next, be honest about where you are in life, your age, your physical abilities, your educational level, your skill level and your talents. Are you equipped to do the things you'd like to do? If education or physical abilities are lacking, how close can you get to what you want to do?

I once had a client who wanted to own his own bed and breakfast, but he had almost no experience in the hospitality field. We worked on understanding his skills, education and talents, and we searched for a job in hospitality where they would transfer. Just being in that industry will give him a wealth of information to later help him open his own establishment to "put heads in beds."

If you haven't already done so, go back to "The Metamorphosis" and work the exercises. When you've completed those, answer the following questions:

(1) What was I doing the last time I lost track of time?

_____

_____

(2) What was it about the activity that caused me to forget about time?

_____

_____

(3) What do I daydream about when there are no restrictions to be considered?

_____

_____

(4) What am I usually doing when I have these daydreams? (In other words, what activity do you most want to escape from?)

_____

_____

(5) If I could choose any lifestyle, what would that be?

_____

_____

(6) Read the sentences below. Put a check mark in the box beside the two statements that appeal to you the most. Put an X in the box beside the two that appeal to you the least. (*Target Training International and Bill J. Bonnstetter granted permission to use the information below.*)

(a) I value money and a return on my investment. I give freely of my time and talents, but I want and expect a return on my investment. I tend to evaluate things for their utility and economic return.

(b) I live by a system of beliefs, and I like unity and order in my life and following proven procedures rather than quick fixes.

(c) I enjoy form and harmony. I seek creative expression. My philosophy is to stop and smell the roses because life is not a dress rehearsal.

(d) I am generous with my time, talents and resources. I believe in putting others before self. I enjoy seeing others develop their full potential. I will champion a worthy cause.

(e) I enjoy positions of leadership and advancing my position. I can plan and carry out a winning strategy, attain and use power to accomplish my purpose. So bring it on! I want the highest position with lots of influence.

(f) I enjoy the pursuit of knowledge. I collect seminar brochures and want to sign up for them all! There is no such thing as too many books. Give me the hard, cold facts and research.

Let's look at each one of these. The order doesn't really matter for this exercise.

(a) If you picked this as one of your most appealing, you are utilitarian and like to be acknowledged and rewarded for your work. Maybe a career in sales, investing or accounting is right for you. You would not like to be in a position or work with a company where your efforts are not recognized. Going to work for a charity is not for you.

Here are two quotes you'll probably identify with:

Money swore an oath that nobody who didn't love it should ever have it.

~~Irish proverb

If you aren't getting faster, stronger and smarter, you are getting slower, weaker and dumber.

~~Anonymous

(b) If this was one of your top selections, you're traditional and like to work in an atmosphere where tried and true rules and regulations are in place and practiced. You probably enjoy having a religious life. Working for someone who is unethical is not for you. You need a position with structure and guidance.

Your quotes:

Better to die standing than to live on your knees.

~~Yiddish proverb

I believe in a force more powerful than myself.

~~Anonymous

(c) If this was one of your most appealing, you are aesthetic and may well have an artistic bent ranging from architecture to zoology. Relationships mean more to you than the task at hand. You need to be in an atmosphere that is pleasing to both the eye and the spirit. I'd say police work is out for you.

Quotes for you:

A wildflower on the mountain top would not change places with a rose in a garden.
~~Armenian proverb

Take time to smell the roses...you only live once, so enjoy it while you can.
~~Anonymous

(d) If you picked this one, you are social and you may well enjoy working for a charity or a nonprofit organization. You would make a good teacher or coach. An atmosphere of solitude is not for you. I'd avoid the lone guard position at the local shipyard.

Your own quotes:

The best passion is compassion.
~~Jamaican proverb

What goes around, comes around.
~~A modern-day golden rule

(e) If you selected this one, you are individualistic and need a position where you can be visible, or at least in charge of projects. Does the term "entrepreneur" ring your bell? You don't mind taking the blame or basking in praise. You say, "No pain, no gain, no guts, no glory." The last desk in the back of the room in the accounting department in the basement will send you screaming into the streets.

Here are your two very own quotes:

Victory has a hundred fathers. Defeat is an
orphan.
~~Chinese proverb

The road to success is filled with many obstacles.
~~Anonymous

(f) If you chose this one, you are theoretical and want to learn all you can about a topic. You might consider a job in research or a position in education or training. If you're expected to make quick decisions and shoot from the hip, you will probably shoot yourself in the foot.

Your personal quotes:

Not to know is bad, not to wish to know is worse.
~~African proverb

If you aren't prepared, don't expect to win.
~~Anonymous

Whichever two you selected as being your LEAST appealing, stay away from positions or environments where these attributes are prevalent. The two least appealing will not cause you to lose track of time, and you can kiss the state of bliss goodbye. These won't lead to the dream career you've been looking for, but rather the nightmare that needs avoiding! This is why it's so essential to understand what drives you. The items you selected are what get you out of bed in the morning and lead you to action. The ones with an X are poison. The two you did *not* mark at all are situational for you. In other words, depending on the situation you're in, you can call on these attributes and use them to your advantage.

I wanted to be a teacher when I was a child (yes, one of my top attributes is theoretical), and I've finally turned that passion into a career as a trainer. As you've read, my career path took many unrelated twists and turns before arriving where I am today. In college, I studied training, but I also joined professional associations like American Society for Training and Development (ASTD), bought every book I could find on adult training, attended any seminar I could talk my boss into sending me to, and continued learning and improving. Today I have my own training company. Ahhhh, a dream come true!

The game of life is a lot like football. You have to
tackle your problems, block your fears, and score
your points when you get the opportunity.
~~Lewis Grizzard (1947-1994)
Comedian, columnist, author

After you pinpoint your passion, join at least one organization or group that focuses on that area. It will be an opportunity to learn, to meet people with the same interests, and to understand the industry or area better. Almost every field has an association, so it shouldn't be hard to find one.

Don't be a victim of happenstance. When you take control of your life's work, you take control of your life, your environment, the people you associate with, and the tasks you perform. Doing what you love empowers you with more self-confidence, self-respect and self-reliance. And having such a positive sense of self will help prevent your falling prey to victimization. The only time you are allowed to tie your bootstraps is when you tie them around your dream.

When you take charge of your life, there is no
longer a need to ask permission of other people or
society at large. When you ask permission, you give
someone veto power over your life.
~~Geoffrey F. Abert
American author

68

We hold these truths to be self-evident, that all men are created equal, that they are endowed by their Creator with certain unalienable rights, that among these are life, liberty, and the pursuit of happiness.
~~The Declaration of Independence, July 1776

It's official! Even the government says you
have the right to pursue your dreams!

Even though you may want to move forward in your life, you may have one foot on the brakes. In order to be free, we must learn how to let go. Release the hurt. Release the fear. Refuse to entertain your old pain. The energy it takes to hang onto the past is holding you back from a new life. What is it you would let go of today?
~~Mary Manin Morrissey
American author

You gotta untie the bootstraps!

Nobody is stronger, nobody is weaker, than someone who came back. There is nothing you can do to such a person because whatever you could do is less than what has already been done to him. We have already paid the price.
~~Elie Wiesel (1928)
Activist and American (Romanian-born) author

See? What have you got to lose?

The Wright brothers flew right through the smoke screen of impossibility.
~~Charles F. Kettering (1876-1958),
US electrical engineer and inventor

This is what dreams can do.

A pessimist sees the difficulty in every opportunity; an optimist sees the opportunity in every difficulty.
~~Sir Winston Churchill (1874-1965)
British politician

You have the power to CHANGE your attitude.

This above all: to thine own self be true, And it must follow, as the night the day, Thou canst not then be false to any man.
~~William Shakespeare, ibid.
From Hamlet, 3.1.81

Pursue your dream—it is you!

Kites rise highest against the wind, not with it.
~~Sir Winston Churchill, ibid.

While you're pulling on your bootstraps,
push against all those obstacles in your way.

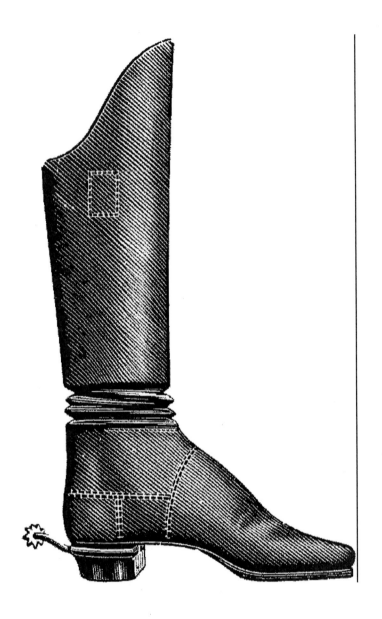

Step 5: Embrace Error Messages—
Change Is Seldom Faultless

Everyone makes mistakes; the trick is to learn from them. People who continually make the same mistake over and over have not learned anything. The old saying, "Insanity is doing the same thing over and over and expecting different results," means that no progress can be made until we learn to take the valuable lessons of our mistakes and turn them into a catalyst for change.

Many people stay in their ruts because they fear change more than they fear the rut! At least in the rut, they know what to expect. This is often even true of people who are being abused—at least they know when to duck. When you are in an environment of unknowns, you have to *learn* when and what to duck. But once you understand that life is a series of changes, your fear of the unknown and of making mistakes will diminish.

Change makes up our lives—it happens every day. People are born, people die, people make money, people file for bankruptcy, people get married, people get divorced, people start a new job, people get fired or quit, new buildings are built, old buildings are torn down, new companies are formed, other companies fold, the boss you had yesterday goes to work at another company today, and on and on and on. All of these events create change, and mistakes are made, but the planet keeps turning no matter who makes what mistake.

Confidence comes not from always being right but-
from not fearing to be wrong.
~~Peter T. McIntyre (1910-1995)
New Zealand artist

The best way to deal with change is to take it on slowly. Humans, for the most part, are creatures of habit, so begin by making subtle changes to your routine. Take an alternate route to work. Go somewhere different for lunch. Make it a point to meet two new people every week. Change your reading habits. Change the way you talk to yourself and others. Change the way you think about yourself. If you make mistakes along the way, just correct them as you go. In other words, subtly change your changes.

Remember that you are not allowed to verbally beat yourself up over mistakes you make while changing. Tell yourself something like, "Well, that didn't work. Let's see how I can do this differently next time to get the results I'm looking for." As Reverend Robert H. Schuller says, "It's better to do something imperfectly than to do nothing flawlessly." Believe me, you'll never be alone in the mistake department. Would you believe this to be true if you heard it from "the smartest person in the world"? Marilyn vos Savant has the highest IQ ever recorded—288. When a writer asked her why we (even the brightest among us) can't stop making mistakes, she replied:

When we are born, we know virtually nothing. To learn anything, we must explore new territory. So, unless we behave like passive receivers of information (like a computer being programmed), or have perfect luck and guess right every time, we will make mistakes. This activity expands when we go to school and retracts after we leave, in the absence of motivation or encouragement.

But in some people, especially those who are inquisitive and bright, the process continues throughout life. They never stop learning—and making mistakes. Others try to avoid error by staying in familiar territory. But life is so short, and the world of learning so vast, that I feel safe in stating that if you do not make mistakes, you don't know much.

~~Marilyn vos Savant
Ask Marilyn, July 24, 2005

If you wait for the ship of perfection to sail your way, you will probably wind up drowning in the undercurrent of what might have been. No one's life, dreams, business or relationship begins at the point of perfection. Indeed, true perfection may *never* show itself.

Striving for excellence motivates you; striving for perfection is demoralizing.

~~Harriet Braiker, PhD (1948-2004)
Clinical psychologist and author

The Wright brothers had 70 attempts under their belts before the first airplane flight was a reality. What if they had never tried, or had quit after the first two or three attempts, for fear of making a mistake? We'd still be traveling across the country in covered wagons to see family and friends.

Thomas Edison experimented with thousands of lightbulb filaments until he developed the one that worked best.

If everyone waited until they could be the perfect parent, our population would be a lot lower than it is now.

In truth, life itself is trial and error. Even Mother Nature has to experiment. Look at some of the sights around you and I'm sure you'll agree!

Do not be too timid and squeamish about your actions. All life is an experiment. The more experiments you make, the better. What if they are a little coarse and you may get your coat soiled or torn? What if you do fail and get fairly rolled in the dirt once or twice? Up again, you shall never be so afraid of a tumble.
~~Ralph Waldo Emerson (1803-1882)
American author, poet, philosopher

The greatest mistake you can make is to continually fear you will make one.
~~Elbert Hubbard (1856-1915)
American author, from A Message to Garcia

Hey, your bootstraps don't even have to match!
Just PULL!

I've always felt it was not up to anyone else to make me give my best.
~~Akeem Olajuwon (1963)
American basketball player

See? It's all inside!

What we see depends mainly on what we look for.
~~Sir John Lubbock (1803-1865)
Astronomer and mathematician

There's that attitude thing again.
Do you look for misery?
Do you look for excuses where there are none?
Do you look to the past instead of the present?
Do you look past the present to a gloomy future?
Stay focused on the PRESENT!

The most important thing about motivation is goal setting. You should always have a goal.
~~Francie Larrieu Smith (1952)
American track and field star

Oh, come on, you knew goal-setting would show up eventually! If you don't know where you're going, you're going to wind up knee-deep in something smelly.

This time, like all times, is a very good one if we but know what to do with it.
~~Ralph Waldo Emerson, ibid.

You should be pulling on those bootstraps!
DO IT NOW!

Everyone is trying to accomplish something big, not realizing that life is made up of little things.
~~Frank A. Clark (1911)
American author

This is where a lot of people get their bootstraps tied up in knots. They think they must accomplish something as big as all outdoors or it doesn't count. The trick is to do something—no matter how small— toward your dream each and every day.
That's progress.

We do not what we ought; what we ought not, wedo; and lean upon the thought that chance will bring us through; but our own acts, for good or ill, are mightier powers.
~~Empedocles (C. 450 BCE)
Italian philosopher

Actions speak louder than words … so do something, even if it's wrong. Remember, we learn from our mistakes.

The character that takes command in moments of-crucial choices has already been determined. It has been determined by a thousand other choices made earlier in seemingly unimportant moments. It has been determined by all the "little" choices of years past—by all those times when the voice of conscience was at war with the voice of tempta-tion—whispering the lie that "it doesn't really matter." It has been determined by all the day-to-day decisions made when life seemed easy and cri-ses seemed far away—the decisions that, piece by piece, bit by bit, developed habits of discipline or laziness, habits of self-sacrifice or of self-indul-gence, habits of duty and honor and integrity—or dishonor and shame.

~~Ronald Reagan (1911-1004)
40th US President

Character isn't inherited. One builds it daily by the-way one thinks and acts, thought by thought, ac-tion by action. If one lets fear or hate or anger take possession of the mind, they become self-forged chains.

~~Helen Gahagan Douglas (1900-1980)
Actress, politician, activist, public speaker

Again, proof that our lives are built one minute,
one decision, and one action at a time, every single day.

Over a lifetime, the actual pain of feeling inconsequential, irrelevant and inconspicuous is far greater than the imagined pain of an occasional rejection.

~~Anonymous

Failure is only the opportunity to more intelligently begin again.

~~Henry Ford (1863-1947)
American automobile manufacturer

Aim for success, not perfection. Never give up your right to be wrong, because then you will lose the ability to learn new things and move forward with your life. Remember that fear always lurks behind perfectionism. Confronting your fears and allowing yourself the right to be human can, paradoxically, make you a happier and more productive person.

~~Dr. David M. Burns
Professor of psychiatry and behavioral
sciences at Stamford University

Hmmmm, I think we should put that in the
inalienable rights section of the Constitution.

Those who dare to fail miserably can achieve greatly.

~~John F. Kennedy (1917-1963)
35th US President

Step 6: Fight the Fear Factor—
Be the Hero of Your Life

I didn't get my driver's license until I was 25, but I dreamed about driving. And in my driving dreams, I did everything exactly as it should be done. After I took lessons and got my license, I never had that dream again. But every time I even *thought* about getting behind the wheel, I became nauseated. Sometimes I would tell myself to give up, it's no use, I can't do this, it's just too scary. This went on for so long that I began to think it would never go away. Even though learning to drive had been a dream of mine for a long time, I was ready to give it up out of fear.

Oh, I had *lots* of fears! I was afraid to stand up for myself because my husband might divorce me. (As it turned out, I divorced him!) I was afraid to look for a job, because I had no experience, talent or skills. I was afraid of water, so I couldn't jump in the deep end of the pool during my swimming lessons. Fear of rejection kept me from applying to college. My list goes on and on.

Understand that fear has a couple of components. One tells us that something is bad, dangerous or threatening: "Be careful," "Be aware," "Watch out." This component represents rational warnings to us. Be careful, if you touch a hot pan, you'll get burned. Be aware, something is not right with a situation. Find out what it is and avoid or work around it. Watch out, there are cars coming. This component serves us daily as a guiding tool.

The second element tells us that something is catastrophic: "This will ruin you." This component comes from the value you place on a situation. For example, the fear I had that my husband would divorce me if I ever spoke my mind, got a job or challenged him in any way. The institution of marriage meant a great deal to me, especially my own. But it also represented a large part of my self-worth. What could be worse than divorce? What could be worse than having the one you love not return that love? What could be worse than rejection?

We all know that there are many worse things in life than these: the death of a child, discovering you have terminal cancer, or any other of life's horrors. Even worse, however, is never learning to love and respect yourself, because if you have that, you can get through anything. But once you encase a situation in the irrational component of fear, you're lost. Because you have sold yourself the belief that your life is a catastrophe, an Elizabethan tragedy, a soap opera. A life with rational fear is none of these.

Fear and anger are Siamese twins, and they support each other. There are four levels of anger. Usually with overt anger, the fear level is low. When the fear level gets a little higher, the anger becomes passive/aggressive behavior—the "I can get you, but you can't get me back" syndrome. When the fear level gets higher than that, suppression results—the conscious exclusion of "unacceptable" thoughts or desires. At the highest level of fear, the anger becomes repression—the classical defense mechanism that protects you from impulses or ideas that would cause anxiety by preventing them from becoming conscious.

Keep in mind that people who are always angry have an addiction: they need to control something or someone. Don't let that someone be you. Fear and anger are dream killers. They must be conquered.

The mind and heart can't entertain two emotions at the same time, and you have the power to choose the positive one! Allow yourself to challenge your own anger so you can take back your power. How? First, let's determine who is controlling your life. Honestly answer the following questions Yes or No:

(1)   Do you always follow the rules? _____

(2)   Do you ever question the sensibility of rules? _____

81

(3)   Is being viewed as obedient important to you? _____

(4)   Do you feel guilty deviating from the rules?   _____

(5)   Do you find yourself engaging in soothing behavior when conflict arises?
_____

(6)   Are you unable to directly communicate your own frustration or upset
feeling ? _____

(7)   Do you feel you need to be in a romantic relationship to be safe and
secure? _____

(8)   Do you have a low tolerance to being alone and enjoying your own
company? _____

(9)   Does having total financial and emotional responsibility for yourself
frighten you?   _____

(10)   Do you feel you are living your life to the fullest? _____

(11)   Will you often do things you don't want to do in order to avoid
disapproval? _____

(12)   Do people's opinions about you concern you? _____

(13)   Do you have difficulty saying No? _____

(14)   Is it very important that you do not disappoint others? _____

(15)   Do you feel guilty when you disappoint someone? _____

(16)   Are you persuaded easily? _____

(17)   In a professional situation, do you have difficulty speaking out? _____

(18)   Is it ever difficult for you to express a different point of view?   _____

(19)   Do you avoid being viewed as a wave-maker? _____

(20)   Do you see being a wave-maker as being a troublemaker?_____

Answering Yes to three or more of these questions indicates that you are not in control of your life. You are, instead, letting others have your personal power.

Here are five steps to taking back your own power:

Step 1. Realize you have the power of choice. Unless you live in some Third World country or are chained in a basement somewhere, you have the power to choose. To illustrate just how powerful choice can be, do the following exercise from the book *Psychological Self-Help* by clinical psychologist Dr. Clayton Tucker-Ladd, found at http://mentalhelp.net/psyhelp/chap15/chap15e.htm.

Begin this experience by completing these sentences with several responses:

(1) I had to _____

(2) I can't _____

(3) I need _____

(4) I'm afraid to_____

(5) I'm unable to_____

Do this before you do the second half below, or you are likely to miss the point.

Now, go back and try substituting these words for the five beginning above:

(1) Instead of *I had to*, write *I chose to...* (whatever you filled in above).

(2) Instead of *I can't,* write *I won't...* (whatever you filled in above).

(3) Instead of *I need,* write *I want...* (whatever you filled in above).

(4) Instead of *I'm afraid to,* write *I'd like to...* (whatever you filled in above).

(5) Instead of *I'm unable to*, write *I'm unwilling to work hard enough to...* (whatever you filled in above).

The answers you give here will give you a large clue as to whether or not you are taking responsibility for your own decisions and, consequently, your own power and life.

Step 2. Ask yourself, "Am I afraid of success?" This may seem strange, but it's a prevalent fear for many people. In her book, *Overcoming the Fear of Success,* Martha Friedman tells the story of a gentleman who was asked if he had always wanted to be a songwriter. He said, "No, I wanted to be a pianist." He went on to say that the reason he had not become a pianist was that his folks couldn't afford piano lessons, and that he wrote songs to make money for his family. Then he was asked why he hadn't pursued his dream after he became rich and famous. He replied, "For some unknown reason, I kept burning my fingers."

The procrastination crutch gets leaned on a lot here. Dr. Gail Saltz, a psychoanalyst in private practice, states that some people use procrastination as a tool to avoid success: "I'm afraid to be successful because people will envy me or see me as a threat, and then I'll lose them."

She asks people to deliberate the following: "Consider the problems your procrastination creates vs. what you think you get out of it. (Example: 'I like being a victim, but that means I never get ahead in life.')" Read more about procrastination and how to overcome it in her article "How to Get Unstuck Now!" in *Parade* magazine, March 20, 2005, Pages 6-8.

Do you sabotage your own ability to become successful? See if you can relate to any of the following questions:

(1)   Are you a perfectionist?
(2)   Do you procrastinate?
(3)   Are you afraid of making a mistake?
(4)   Do you think being competitive is a negative idea?
(5)   Is it hard for you to accept compliments?
(6)   Do you feel like a fraud?
(7)   Do you downplay your successes?
(8)   Are you frequently late for appointments?
(9)   Do you enjoy feeling bad or depressed?
(10)   Are you unable to have a successful intimate relationship?

Yes answers here indicate that you do have a fear of success. Taking each of the questions to which you answered Yes and turning them into Nos (did you ever think you would be told to turn something into a negative?) will get you over your fear of success and soon you will develop your personal power and be embracing, even chasing, success!

Step 3. Tell yourself that you deserve to have your own power. Many people don't celebrate their birthdays because they feel they didn't even deserve to be born, much less have any power. If you are alive and breathing, you deserve to have and exercise your own power.

Step 4. Be accountable. No one can take responsibility for developing your personal power. This is your job. I have taken many motivational/self-help classes and then failed to implement the ideas and suggestions I sometimes paid money to hear. No one can do this for you. Only you can take the actions necessary to make the needed changes in your life.

Step 5. Embrace truth. Accept the truth about who you are, the person you want to be, and what you must do to achieve that goal.

Be brutally honest about your fears and how you use them as excuses to keep you from moving forward. Quit lying to yourself about your inability to develop your power. Be honest about your positive attributes. Know that you can cultivate them to propel you toward your goal of attaining personal power.

Where fear is, happiness is not.
~~Lucius Annacus (c. 4BC-65AD)
Roman playwright

Let's look at a simple process to conquer fear:

(1) Clearly identify the fear you want to conquer.

(2) Analyze why you have this fear. Are you afraid of failing? Afraid that you will forget what you have to do? Afraid you have nothing to say that anyone wants to hear? You may think, "If I do this, I'll think of things to be afraid of that I hadn't even thought about before!" That's OK too, because if you think of what may go wrong, you can prepare to overcome these things if they *do* go wrong.

For example, if you are afraid of failing, you will never know whether it's a valid feeling unless you try to do the thing you fear. If you do fail, just try again until you conquer the task. If you're afraid of forgetting what you were going to say, have notes with you. If you think no one wants to hear what you have to say, make sure you are speaking to someone who *will* be interested.

(3) Prepare. If you are afraid to speak in public, you could read a book on presentation skills, join Toastmasters International, or take a speaking class at your local college. Some colleges even offer inexpensive continuing education classes to the general public for no course credit. Of course, if you have the money, you can use the services of any number of businesses, such as Dale Carnegie, that teach public speaking. Or a less expensive idea is to hire a personal coach. A coach can provide private, individualized, customized training for you. Having done your homework on what you want to pursue will get you through bouts of self-doubt.

One important key to success is self-confidence.An important key to self-confidence is preparation.
~~Arthur Ashe (1943-1993)
American tennis champion

---

(4) Study other people, especially those you want to emulate, doing what you fear. Someone has probably already done whatever you dread. Find that person and watch and learn. Then do what they do.

(5) Use positive visualization. See yourself doing the thing you fear and see yourself doing it well. Mental practice has been proven through scientific research to be highly effective in helping people achieve goals. It has to do with the old adage "Practice makes perfect." There is no guarantee that the outcome will occur or be perfect. According to http://www.tenzone.u-net/psych/psyvis.htm, it works like this:

> "Research has shown that imagined performance generates
> appropriate muscle responses. It's not clear why, but the
> implication is that imagined performance really does exercise
> much of the brain's motor function—it isn't all imagination."

In other words, mental rehearsal helps you to prepare for and deal with possible situations.

Dr. Robert Yourell, a licensed psychotherapist, http//www. psychinovations.com/mrehears.htm, gives us a step-by-step method to mentally rehearse: "Use this exercise to improve performance in just about anything, including coping with an upsetting person, public speaking, sports, saving your marriage, etc., etc.

Step I: Set Up
(1) Pick the situation in which you want to perform at your best.

(2) Think: What results do you want? What kind of performance
   equals excellence?

87

(3) Ask yourself, "*When* have I ever felt anything like that, or like some part of that?

Step II: Get the Right State

(1) Ask yourself, "What would be the best way I could possibly *feel*
to be at my best in this situation?"

(2) Ask yourself, "What words or phrases express the ways I want to feel in the situation?"

(3) Ask yourself, "*When* have I ever felt anything like that, or like some part of that?"

Step III: Amplify the State

(1) Start getting that ideal feeling by thinking of past experiences and words and phrases.

(2) *Amplify* the feelings, just like adjusting a television: brightness, volume, intensity, whatever.

(3) If the feelings are weak, *describe* them to yourself with words like "confident, posed, clear," and go to the next step.

Step IV: The Rehearsal

(1) *Imagine the situation* as if you were watching yourself in a movie.

(2) Imagine that you are fully in that ideal feeling, *as shown* by your face, posture, movement, and voice.

(3) If you don't like how the fantasy goes, *rewind* it a bit and adjust it until you like what you see.

Special tip: If the fantasy seems to have a mind of its own, you have probably found some deeper resistance to change. If so, STOP right there and really focus your highest intentions on changing it to be positive. ***Don't get stuck in anger or being a victim,*** (emphasis mine) for example, if you run into too much trouble, coaching or counseling might be your best bet.

Step V: The Special Ending: This part is very important!
    This part of the process turns off the anxiety your primitive
brain areas produce in this situation. This is critical to changing
your physical reaction and making room for your creative, focused
confidence.

**This process isn't intended to build unrealistic expectations, or to
use magic.** It is designed to improve your readiness for the real situation.

Choice 1: Understanding. This ending is good when you are dealing with
someone who upsets, angers or hurts you. In your imagination, have them express a perfect understanding of your highest positive motives and intentions. In other words, they show that they really understand why you are doing
what you are doing, and they explain it to you really well. Push past your anger
and let go of your usual ways of picturing this.

Choice 2: Winning. *If performance is the number one priority*, as with
sports, sales, testimony, etc., imagine the perfect outcome. Really get into the
details of it. For example, see yourself at your best, then getting the trophy. [A
"trophy" can be a real item or an intangible thing like "winning" self- respect.]

Guidelines: Mental rehearsal is an art. You increase its value by advancing
your skills, and aligning your motives. Get coaching or training from an expert.
Be honest and accurate about the benefits, and about what your past patterns
tell you that you need.

- Do this once a day, or whenever the issue is on your mind, like at a
  stoplight. If you're too busy, do it just before bedtime.
- If you go to sleep easily, do it sitting up.
- To stay on track, refer to this sheet as you go.
- Don't just try it once. Keep the faith and keep at it for a month. See
  how you feel!

Fight the Fear Factor-
Be the Hero of Your Life

- Keep refining your idea of excellent performance, and keep expand ing your sense of the ideal states for these situations.
- You may be surprised at how much you can learn about what these two things really mean."

Now back to our steps for conquering fear:

Step VI: Do what you fear at every opportunity. Practice makes perfect. For instance, if you're afraid of speaking out, begin with the simple act of asking a question in a meeting, or giving your opinion about the topic being discussed. The size of the meeting doesn't matter—it could be just you and one other person. Patricia Fripp, a well-known professional speaker, says, "Any talking outside the bedroom is public speaking." So you see, you have actually been "speaking in public" all your life.

These steps will help you overcome most any fear. Living in constant dread only gives us the darkest of perspectives on life. It prevents us from painting our canvas of life with living color.

It is a miserable state of mind to have few things
to desire and many things to fear.
~~Sir Francis Bacon (1561-1626)
Renaissance author, courtier,
father of deductive reasoning

The only thing we have to fear is fear itself—
nameless, unreasoning, unjustified terror which
paralyzes needed efforts to convert retreat into
advance.
~~Franklin Delano Roosevelt (1933-1945)
32nd US President
From his inaugural address, March 1933

It is hard to fail, but it is worse never to have tried to succeed. In this life, we get nothing save by effort.
~~Theodore Roosevelt (1858-1919)
26th US President

Yet another Roosevelt. Wise folks, huh?

Even death is not to be feared by one who has lived wisely.
~~Buddha (Siddhartha Gautama) (c.563–483 BC)
Indian mystic, founder of Buddhism

For all sad words of tongue and pen, the saddest are these: It might have been.
~~John Greenleaf Whittier (1807-1892)
Quaker poet

What is needed, rather than running away or-controlling or suppressing or any other resistance,is understanding fear; that means watch it, learn about it, come directly into contact with it. We are to learn about fear, not how to escape from it.
~~Jiddu Krishnamurti (1895-1986)
Eastern Indian philosopher

If you fear making anyone mad, then you ultimately probe for the lowest common denominator of human achievement.
~~James Earl "Jimmy" Carter, Jr. (1924)
39th US President

Courage is not the absence of fear, but rather the judgment that something else is more important than fear.

~~Ambrose Redmoon
(aka James Neil Hollingsworth) (1933-1996)
American writer and rock music manager

Your life and your dreams are far more important than fear—
trust me on this!

I have not ceased being fearful, but I have ceased to let fear control me. I have accepted fear as a part of life—specifically the fear of change, the fear of the unknown—and I have gone ahead despite the pounding in my heart that says, "Turn back, turn back, you'll die if you venture too far."

~~Erica Jong (1942)
American poet, novelist

Let's not lose fear totally.
It serves a purpose by giving you energy,
anticipation and heightened awareness.
Make your fear work *for* you, not against you.

If you listen to your fears, you will die never knowing what a great person you might have been.
~~Robert H. Schuller, ibid.

Anxiety is a thin stream of fear trickling through the mind. If encouraged, it cuts a channel into which all other thoughts are drained.
~~Robert Albert Bloch (1917)
American screen writer, "Psycho"

If you were afraid to go in the shower after watching *Psycho,*
you know that fear and anxiety are only
mind games we play with ourselves.

Fear cannot be banished, but it can be calm and without panic; and it can be mitigated by reason and evaluation.
~~Vannevar Bush (1890-1974)
American electrical engineer and physicist

You see, no one is going to jump into your shower
and plunge a knife in your back if you pursue your dreams,
or even if you make a mistake *while* pursuing them.

He who is not everyday conquering some fear has not learned the secret of life.
~~Ralph Waldo Emerson, ibid.

Keep the faith, baby.

Fear is a tyrant and a despot, more terrible than the rack, more potent than the snake.
~~Edgar Wallace (1875-1932)
British novelist, playwright and journalist,
from The Clue of the Twisted Candle

Jeez, there's a motivating graphic if ever there was one.

I must not fear. Fear is the mind-killer. Fear is the little-death that brings total obliteration. I will face my fear. I will permit it to pass over me and through me. And when it has gone past, I will turn the inner eye to see its path. Where the fear has gone, there will be nothing. Only I will remain.
~~Frank Herbert (1920-1986)
American author, from Dune

You will, you must, survive your fears.
They cannot harm you.

Fears are educated into us and can, if we wish, be educated out.
~~Karl A. Menninger (1893-1990)
American psychiatrist

Step 7: Give up Guilt—
It's Not Your Fault

Well, sometimes guilt is your fault, and sometimes that's OK. The guilt you feel from having done something ethically wrong or unfair, if judged rationally, is good. That type of guilt keeps us on the right side of moral. But guilt based on things other people do—or events totally outside our control—is unhealthy.

Guilt can originate because of our own perceptions, because we project our inner feelings to the world around us. So guilt, or the feeling of wrongness, comes from within us, not from any external source. It's the way abuse victims devalue themselves. Usually, however, we feel guilt because we've done something that someone ELSE doesn't like and has told us is wrong.

Perception is a choice. We choose how we perceive the world. For example, I recently met a woman who had legally divorced her husband, but the husband was still living in the house. He had no job and "no place else to go." When I asked the woman why this situation existed, she said, "Well, he was abused as a child and he makes me feel guilty about abandoning him like his family did." Here we have two people making choices about how they perceive their lives. The husband has made the choice to not let go of his past and move on with his life. He is, in essence, saying that to "throw him out of the house" is wrong because of his childhood. The wife has made the choice to allow this man to project the guilt of his choice onto her. She chose to accept his guilt with him and allow him to do nothing to improve his life.

Give up Guilt-
It's Not Your Fault

Gerald G. Jampolsky, MD, tells us in his book, *Good-Bye to Guilt* (Bantam Books, 1985), "When we perceive others through the eyes of guilt, we are likely to engage in projection. Projection is the mechanism by which we deny responsibility for, and externalize, a thought or feeling we are experiencing—such as guilt—by holding someone else responsible for it."

The "someone" can be anyone in our lives—a relative, an intimate, or just the guy who sells car insurance. Ralph Waldo Emerson said it well:

Why should we assume the faults of our friend, or wife, or father, or child, because they sit around our hearth, or are said to have the same blood? All men have my blood, and I have all men's. Not for that will I adopt their petulance or folly, even to the extent of being ashamed of it. But your isolation must not be mechanical, but spiritual, that is, must be elevation. At times the whole world seems to be in conspiracy to importune you with empathic trifles. Friend, client, child, sickness, fear, want, charity, all knock at once at the closet door and say, "Come out unto us." But keep thy state; come not into their confusion. The power men possess to annoy me, I give them by a weak curiosity. No man can come near me but through my act. What we love that we have, but by desire we bereave ourselves of the love.

The phrase "The power men possess to annoy me, I give them by a weak curiosity" speaks volumes. We give others the ability to "annoy" us, to make us feel unloved and guilty. We give others permission to affect our perceptions in life.

It's important to keep our perceptions in check and to take back our ability to rationally judge our actions. Excessive guilt can inhibit our social selves, prevent us from enjoying life, create fear and worry, cause us to alter our thought processes, let us behave irrationally, and even lead to suicide.

Generally, guilt can make us and those around us miserable.

How can you overcome irrational guilt? Look carefully at the event you're feeling guilty over. Take a walk by yourself, or take a trip, or write about it in a journal. You can also talk with someone whose opinion you trust—a noninvested third party. Talking with your mother-in-law or your sister's best friend is probably not a good idea.

(1) Be honest about who has what responsibility. You may bear some and the other person may bear some. Be realistic about who owns what in the development and ongoing status of the situation.

(2) Ask yourself, "How have I contributed to making this condition worse?" At this point, we are only concerned with *your* contribution because you can only acknowledge and change your own thoughts, feelings and behaviors.

(3) Ask yourself, "How is the guilt I feel changing the situation?"

(4) Ask yourself, "What positive emotions, thoughts or feelings has my guilt brought into my life and these circumstances?"

(5) Ask yourself, "How would this change if I had no guilt? Would it stay the same, get better, or become worse?"

(6) Ask yourself, "Have my guilt feelings brought about what I want?"

(7) Ask yourself, "How can this situation or problem be logically solved?"

You want to strive for a win/win, of course, but that may not always be possible. The main goal is to get you out of the situation and over your notions of guilt. Don't let a spouse, parent or member of society make you feel guilty for trying to change your life. Their opinions and ideas are their problem, not yours.

Forgive yourself for whatever it is you think you did to deserve such guilt. If someone else is involved, forgive him or her. In our example above of the husband and wife, he needs to forgive his family for mistreating him. The wife needs to forgive her husband for being unable to cope. Forgiveness, in this instance, does not mean they must stay together. The act of forgiving will allow them both to get on with their lives, get past the past, and let go of their guilt. Once you let go, you will feel like a dam has broken as the flood gates release the pent-up, unhealthy emotions that have been preventing you from leading a full life.

Learn to say No. Being able to say No will free you emotionally and intellectually. Our emotional guilt comes from the feeling that we are letting someone down by saying No. If we say No, this person will be offended. Maybe they will, but I'm sure they have had, and will have, many other disappointments in life, and they will survive. So we need to say No in the least offensive way possible by offering our "rejected" friend another source. For example, let's say I have asked you to help me collate and bind some data for a presentation I have to give. You can say No and then immediately follow-up with a suggestion: "No, Diane, I don't have the time, but I know that Roger may be able to help you." (Be very sure Roger doesn't mind your volunteering him!) Or, "No, Diane, I can't do that, but I know that new office supply place down on Spring Road offers that service rather inexpensively." Did you notice what was missing? You didn't offer any excuses as to why you don't have time or why you can't help me right now. Offering excuses weakens your case and makes you sound as if you feel guilty saying No.

Here's the intellectual part. Saying No is a big time saver. You can't get caught up in performing deeds for other people at the risk of getting yourself off track in pursuing your own goals, deadlines and duties. It is nice to be able to lend a hand once in a while, but when you fall into the "I'm just a girl who can't say No" trap, you become a victim at your own hand. Saying No is another way to take back your personal power, your time and your emotions.

Guilt is perhaps the most painful companion of death.
~~Coco Chanel (1883-1971)
French fashion designer

Successful guilt is the bane of society.
~~Publilus Syrus (1st century BC)
Roman author

Guilt is the very nerve of sorrow.
~~Horace Bushnell (1802-1876)
American Congregational minister

The sense of inferiority and the sense of guilt are exceedingly difficult to distinguish.
~~Sigmund Freud (1856-1939)
Father of psychoanalysis

It is quite gratifying to feel guilty if you haven't done anything wrong: how noble! Whereas it is rather hard, and certainly depressing, to admit guilt and to repent.
~~Hannah Arendt (1906-1975)
Political theorist

Step 8: Be Persistent— Shake it Off and Step Up

I have given up many times in life. Why I gave up doesn't really matter, because I don't have any good reasons. I simply gave up. I often wonder how much farther I would be in my life and business if I hadn't.

About 20 years ago, I wrote a children's book entitled *Rudolph Gets Fired!* It got rejection letters on top of rejection letters, and I didn't even attempt to write another book until 2003! Even when my editor returned the book to me after its second editing, I was so discouraged that I couldn't look at it again for several months. But in this instance I *did* persist and, voila, I became an author.

We let many things get in our way and distract us from our goals, like my lack of self-confidence deterred me. Other people had the "secret" and I didn't. In looking at situations a little more logically, however, I discovered that people with half the talent and experience were doing the things I wanted to do, and I knew I could do them better. Each time I gave up on my dreams, it put me farther behind those who had the persistence to keep on going against all the odds. If there was a secret, that was it.

The bad news is that we are not born with a pocketful of persistence. The good news is that we can train ourselves to be persistent. Napoleon Hill, in his classic book, *Think and Grow Rich* (Fawcett Crest Books, 1960), lists eight elements of persistence:

(1) Purpose: "Knowing what one wants is the first, and perhaps the most important, step toward the development of persistence. A strong motive forces one to surmount many difficulties."

(2) Desire: "It is comparatively easy to acquire and maintain persistence in pursuing the object of intense desire."

(3) Self-Reliance: "Belief in one's ability to carry out a plan encourages one to follow the plan through with persistence."

(4) Precise Plan: "Organized plans, even though they may be weak and entirely impractical, encourage persistence."

(5) Accurate Knowledge: "Knowing that one's plans are sound, based upon experience or observation, encourages persistence; 'guessing' instead of 'knowing' destroys persistence." (This factor will help you persevere when the idea of giving up crawls into your brain.)

(6) Cooperation: "Sympathy, understanding and harmonious cooperation with others tend to develop persistence." (Can you say "support group"?)

(7) Willpower: "The habit of concentrating one's thoughts upon the building of plans for the attainment of a definite purpose leads to persistence."

(8) Good Habits: "Persistence is the direct result of habit. The mind absorbs and becomes a part of the daily experiences upon which it feeds. Fear, the worst of all enemies, can be effectively cured by forced repetition of acts of courage. Everyone who has seen active service in war knows this."

I would add another element: follow-up. Follow-up is persistence's twin. One of my faults is coming on strong and then, poof, everything "evaporates" because I didn't follow up or follow through.

This parable demonstrates how persistence looks in action: A farmer owned an old mule. The mule fell into the farmer's well. The farmer heard the mule saying whatever it is that mules say when they have dropped into someone's well. After carefully assessing the situation, the farmer sympathized with the mule, but decided that neither the well nor the mule was worth saving. So he called his neighbors, told them what had happened, and enlisted their help

103

to haul dirt to bury the mule and put him out of his misery. As you can imagine, the mule was not happy about this plan.

As the farmer and his neighbors began shoveling dirt into the well, the mule noticed that he could just shake the dirt off his back and step up onto it. (This is not your ordinary mule!) So the mule did this, blow after blow. The dirt would hit his back and he would shake it off and step up…shake it off and step up…shake it off and step up! The mule said to himself, "Mule, no matter how painful the blows or how distressing the situation, I will just *shake it off and step up*." (Obviously he read the earlier chapter on self-talk).

Before long, even though the mule was battered and exhausted, he stepped triumphantly over the top of the well! What seemed like it would bury him actually helped him—all because of how he handled adversity.

Life is like that. Many times, what seems to be adversity can actually benefit us if we handle it correctly. So keep facing up to those problems with a positive attitude!

My greatest point is my persistence. I never give up in a match. However down I am, I fight until the last ball. My list of matches shows that I have turned a great many so-called irretrievable defeats into victories.

~~Bjorn Borg (1956)
Swedish tennis player

Failure and I are very well acquainted. I have failed at relationships. Several attempts at businesses have failed—I lost a great deal of money in at least one. I failed to even place in a beauty contest. I failed at completing three previous books. I have failed at getting promotions at work. An acting career failed. A 20-year marriage failed. A selling career failed—OK, dive-bombed. The senior class didn't elect me president of the class even though I thought they liked me.

But I kept trying. Now I am better at relationships, I have a good business, I know better than to enter a beauty pageant, you are reading my second published book, I quit Corporate America (their loss), I gave up selling and am successful at marketing and, as far as the senior class goes, I'll let them have it at our 40th reunion!

The history of the world is full of men who rose to leadership by sheer force of self-confidence, bravery and tenacity.

~~Mahatma Gandhi (1869-1948)
Indian activist and philosopher

Every time you stop pursuing your dream, you lose momentum and precious minutes you could be either working your way toward, or enjoying, success.

A righteous man falls seven times, and rises again.

~~Proverbs 24:16

You are never a loser until you quit trying.

~~Mike Ditka (1939)
American football coach

Many of life's failures are people who did not realize how close they were to success when they gave up.

~~Thomas A. Edison (1847-1931)
American inventor

History has demonstrated that the most notable winners usually encountered heartbreaking obstacles before they triumphed. They won because they refused to become discouraged by their defeats.

~~B. C. Forbes (1880-1954)
Scottish journalist

Be Persistent-
Shake it Off and Step Up

Failures are just lessons we learn. When we take these lessons and apply them to our next attempt, our goals take a giant step toward success.

We can do anything we want to do if we stick to it long enough.
~~Helen Keller (1880-1968)
Deaf and blind woman who became a role model for millions of people

---

Who can doubt the inspiration of Helen Keller? Those of us who have sight, hearing and general good health should be ashamed of our whining, the excuses we give, and the self-pity we lean on in order to not be successful.

I am a slow walker, but I never walk backwards.
~~Abraham Lincoln (1809-1865)
16th US President

Some of us are late bloomers, but that's OK. Look at how Lincoln persisted: At the age of 7, he was forced to work to support his family. At 9, his mother died. At 22, he lost his job as store clerk. At 23, he ran for the state legislature and was soundly defeated. At 26, his business partner died, leaving him with a large debt. The next year, he almost had a nervous breakdown when his best friend died.

At 29, he was defeated in his bid to become House speaker (having finally been elected). Two years later, he lost a bid for presidential elector. By 35, he had been defeated twice for Congress. At 39 (after one term in Congress), he lost his reelection bid. At 41, his 4-year-old son died. At 42, he was rejected as a federal land officer. At 45, he ran for the Senate and lost. At 47, he lost a bid for the vice-presidential nomination (which he didn't even know he was being considered for). At 49, he ran for the Senate again and lost again. But thank heavens he persisted!

I never thought I didn't have a card to play.
~~Jim Lovell (1928)
NASA astronaut

This quote by Jim Lovell is profound. What he is referring to is the circumstances he experienced during the flight of Apollo 13 on April 14, 1970. The flight was beset with major mishaps and malfunctions. Shortly after the booster separation, the center engine was lost. But the crew and the command center on the ground decided it was still a go. After all, they still had four engines left! They shook it off, saying, "We just had our glitch for this mission." They pressed on. Three days into the mission, a defective coil caused an explosion in the oxygen tanks. The ship became uncontrollable (much like life at times) and began to shake. Lovell looked out the window and told Houston that the ship was "venting something." Command determined it was the crew's oxygen. The astronauts were watching their life support stream into space.

What could be worse? But Houston Command said, "Let's work the problem." There was no intention of giving up; they would find Lovell his next card to play. Soon they discovered that the carbon dioxide levels were rising in the craft. Some members of Houston Command gathered up any items they could find that were identical to the ones the space crew had on board. The idea was to "manufacture" a filter. The problem was made worse by the fact that the systems the crew had to hook up did not match. One was square and one was round. Houston did not hesitate. They put together a system and got the instructions to the crew. The crew put the filter together and the carbon dioxide levels dropped.

Both the crew and Houston persisted in solving every problem that came up. If, at any point, either of them had given up, the crew would have been blown to bits. Both the crew and Houston were always willing to look for and play the next card.

You have cards to play, too. Don't ever kid yourself or let anyone else tell you that you don't have choices. Understanding this will always give you another card...sometimes a whole deck!

Bear in mind, if you are going to amount to anything, that your success does not depend upon the brilliance and the impetuosity with which you take hold, but upon the ever-lasting and sanctified bulldoggedness with which you hang on after you have taken hold.

~~Dr. A. B. Meldrum

It is the greatest of all mistakes to do nothing because you can do only a little. Do what you can.

~~Sydney Smith (1771-1845)
English essayist

[Life is] a little like wrestling a gorilla. You don't quit when you're tired, you quit when the gorilla is tired.

~~Robert Strauss (1913-1975)
American actor

Each of us has our own internal gorillas that we fight daily. I thought my daughter's gorilla had won when she divorced after her quickie marriage at 15 and child at 16. But even that wasn't all bad, because she decided to get her GED. After that achievement, she enrolled in our community college, then went on to the local university. Then she dared apply to Emory University. Not only was she accepted, she was #1 in her first graduation class and went back with a double major for her Master's. Was this journey a breeze? Certainly not. It was fraught with crying, stress, long nights and days of study, and thoughts of, "I can't do this!" But she did.

Persistence pays off, and it can take you where you want to go. So to all of you parents with troubled children—keep the faith. Sometimes that light bulb does come on and it burns big and bright.

Nothing in the world can take the place of persistence. Talent will not; nothing is more common than unsuccessful men with talent. Genius will not; unrewarded genius is almost a proverb. Education will not; the world is full of educated derelicts. Persistence and determination alone are omnipotent. The slogan, Press on has solved, and always will solve, the problems of the human race.

~~Calvin Coolidge (1872-1933)
30th US President

Cool, Calvin! This quote is for all of us who compare ourselves to others. It's for those times when we think people who are better educated or more experienced or younger or older or whatever are better than we are. Just keep truckin' and you'll get there!

Step 9: Build Your Self-Esteem and Self-Confidence—Walk Tall

If you just follow the advice given in this book so far, you will boost your self-esteem and self-confidence. I promise you that. But walking tall will make you *feel* tall. Here are a few ways to begin:

Be yourself. Your bootstraps are yours and no one can duplicate them. No one else can be you, and you can't be anyone else, no matter how much you may want to, no matter how hard you try. Some of us are so used to only seeing the negative about ourselves that we fail to appreciate the good. We often miss seeing how our outside (physical) attributes, and our inside (talent) attributes, can be useful or effective in our journey to self-actualization. For example, if you are talkative and boisterous, someone else might see that as enthusiasm. If you are overweight, someone else might see that as being healthy. Make no mistake: The idea is not to deceive ourselves and ignore weaknesses that can be improved, but to see our "faults" from a different perspective. Let's consider physical attributes first.

Recently, on the radio, I heard two disc jockeys asking for opinions about a 12-year-old girl who wanted her mother's permission to get plastic surgery to correct—in the girl's words—her large nose. If the mother gives in and takes her daughter to a plastic surgeon, hopefully the doctor will tell the girl that she is too young for plastic surgery. But then her support group—her family—needs to take things a step further by helping the young lady appreciate her appearance. They could begin by reminding her that many famous people have distinctive noses that helped make them rich and famous! People like singer Barbara Streisand, comedian Jimmy Durante, Egyptian queen Cleopatra, comedian Bob Hope, and let's not forget Pinocchio. OK, Pinocchio wasn't a real person, but his "creator," Carlo Collodi, was real and will forever be famous for his big-nosed boy.

I'm not saying that you shouldn't correct something that's really bothering you or holding you back from being everything you want to be. When I began modeling, my two front teeth were bucked and overlapping. That didn't make for a model's smile, so I had them capped. I also had a mole, or "beauty mark," removed from my face. But singer Aaron Neville has a mole over his eyebrow about four times the size of the one I had, and it hasn't slowed him down! All of the people mentioned, excluding me, have used their physical appearance to help make them more recognizable and famous. People won't forget you and your distinctive look!

Mental attributes may not be so easily recognizable as facial features, but they play just as big a part in helping us to be distinctive. Check off which of the following characteristics apply to you.

- ☐ Ability to develop others
- ☐ Ability to follow directions
- ☐ Ability to handle rejection
- ☐ Ability to integrate past experiences to solve current situations
- ☐ Ability to maintain focus
- ☐ Ability to persuade others to your point of view
- ☐ Ability to take initiative
- ☐ An open mind
- ☐ Attention to detail
- ☐ Common sense
- ☐ Consistency
- ☐ Creativity
- ☐ Emotional control

☐ Freedom from prejudices

☐ Good communicator (including listening)

☐ Good personal relationships

☐ Good planner

☐ Good sense of timing

☐ Good work ethic

☐ Honesty

☐ Intuitive

☐ Organizational skills

☐ Persistence

☐ Personal accountability

☐ Problem solving skills

☐ Realistic expectations

☐ Respect for policies/procedures

☐ Respect for property (yours and others)

☐ Role awareness

☐ Self-awareness

☐ Self-confidence

☐ Self-direction

☐ Self-discipline

☐ Self-management

☐ Sense of commitment

☐ Sense of loyalty

☐ Sensitivity to feelings of others

☐ Sense of humor

☐ Social awareness

Based on materials from Target Training International, with permission

Now take the attributes you have checked off and analyze where they can best be used. For example, sensitivity to feelings of others, problem solving and self-control can all be applied to help you settle conflict. Persistence, the ability to handle rejection and taking initiative will help you bounce back from hard times and maintain your personal resiliency.

The point is that you have many "built-in" qualities that distinguish you and help you gain self-confidence, be proud and walk tall.

Learn to recognize and appreciate your every asset. Once, when I was in therapy, I took some assessments. The doctor told me that one showed I had a good sense of timing. I scoffed and retorted, "Well, big whoop, that will certainly take me far!" He ignored my flippant remark and patiently explained that this was indeed an asset. He said that my sense of timing was what helped me to be a good dancer and that I also seemed to have a good sense of timing about when to broach topics with other people. He explained that a good sense of timing helps one "flow" through and with the environment of everyday events.

I have known artists who dismiss their talent as being nothing and who have no appreciation for their skill. Not everyone can draw, paint a picture, or write a paragraph the way someone else can. If you can't play on the "world stage" to exhibit your talents, explore other avenues. For example, I met a woman who likes to sing jazz. She doesn't feel she can compete in Hollywood or New York, but she wants a business of her own that somehow incorporates jazz. I suggested that she begin promoting her business by speaking to groups (public speaking is a great marketing tool). She can also find a way to incorporate her jazz singing into her presentations. That will help her stand way out in front of the competition. Not only will she be promoting her business, she will be using a talent she loves, and she will be teaching and giving joy to others. Her self-confidence in her talent and her business will grow. If something like that doesn't put your self-esteem and self-confidence on the charts, I don't know what will.

If you are unable to enjoy your talent in one way, there is always an alternative. Remember the old saying, "Those who can't, teach." Teaching your talent to others will definitely give you a sense of pride and increase your self-esteem.

Don't compare yourself to others. One mistake many people make is to let their self-esteem suffer when they are around others who have the same talent. I belong to National Speakers Association, an organization made up of folks who give speeches for a living. At the annual convention, and even in our local chapter, there are people who excel at what they do. Some are quite famous. Some who are not so famous compare themselves to these few and their self-esteem flies out the window. Don't let that happen to you. Always strive to be better, and maybe one day you *will be* famous, but don't make the mistake of dismissing what you have to offer the world.

Use what you have. A colleague of mine was born in East Germany. She grew up behind the wall that the communists built to separate East and West Germany. After the wall was torn down, she came to America, and now she helps others by speaking to groups about tearing down the walls that block us from achieving our goals. Unique? You bet! Even if your life hasn't been unusual or exciting, don't fret. You could still tell stories about how you've learned life's lessons. Or you could write a book like this one. Everyone has unique and/or amusing situations in everyday life. Learn to use what you have and you can build your self-esteem to great heights.

Until you make peace with who you are, you'll never be content with what you have.
~~Doris Mortman
American author

Invest in yourself every day by doing at least one thing toward your goals. Investing this way allows you to "pay yourself first." Invest in yourself financially, too, by saving 10% of everything you make. Even if you can only save $5 a week, you will be ahead of most people. As you save, compound interest kicks in and you earn on the money you save. As you continue to add to your principal, you earn interest on the interest. In time, you will have a nice savings.

Having self-confidence is like that, too. Because you believe in yourself (the principal), others will begin to believe in you (the interest). Doors will start to open for you; you will attract the items, people and opportunities you seek; and individuals who want to help will suddenly show up on your doorstep (compound interest). The more self-confidence you have, the more you will be ready for the events that can spur you along in life and help you reach your goals. When you are ready for these things, they appear as if by magic.

The way to develop self-confidence is to do the thing you fear and get a record of successful experiences behind you. Destiny is not a matter of chance, it is a matter of choice; it is not a thing to be waited for, it is a thing to be achieved.
~~William Jennings Bryant (1860-1925)
American writer, essayist, critic

Self-confidence is the result of a successfully survived risk.
~~Jack R. Gibb, PhD (1916-1995)
Founder of Trust Level Theory (TORI)

We are valued in this world at the rate we desire to be valued.
~~Jean De La Bruyere (1645-1696)
French author

I can testify to this being true. As you now know, most of my life was spent in negative self-talk, depressive thoughts about myself, and the feeling that I had no worth to anyone. Did people take advantage of me? You bet! Those thoughts and feelings got me nowhere. Not until I began to believe in myself did people "suddenly" begin to treat me differently.

Until you value yourself, you will not value your time. Until you value your time, you will not do anything with it.

~~M. Scott Peck, MD (1936)
American author

You may live in an imperfect world, but the frontiers are not closed and the doors are not all shut.

Accept yourself as you are. Otherwise you will never see opportunity. You will not feel free to move toward it; you will feel you are not deserving.

Take the trouble to stop and think of the other person's feelings, his viewpoints, his desires and needs. Think more of what the other fellow wants, and how he must feel.

Begin to imagine what the desirable outcome would be like. Go over these mental pictures and delineate details and refinements. Play them over and over to yourself. [See Step Six: Fight the Fear Factor.]

Within you right now is the power to do things you never dreamed possible. This power becomes available to you just as you can change your beliefs.

Close scrutiny will show that most "crisis situations" are opportunities to either advance or stay where you are.

Low self-esteem is like driving through life with
your hand break on.

Our self-image, strongly held, essentially
determines what we become.

You are embarking on the greatest adventure of
your life—to improve your self-image, to create
more meaning in your life and in the lives of others.
This is your responsibility. Accept it now!

Your most important sale in life is to sell yourself
to yourself.
~~Maxwell Maltz, M.D., F.I.C.S. (1895-1971)
Plastic surgeon and creator of self-improvement
phenomenon, Psycho-Cybernetics

You may think this just applies to people with limited attributes, money, intellect or looks. Not true. There are many people who have great talent but can't accept themselves. It's called the fear of success. Get over it! Discover your talents, find out what you want to do with them, and then grab on to those bootstraps!

Step 10: Become Self-Reliant— Trust Yourself

While all of us need the kind of support group described earlier in this book, you must also develop self-reliance. If you wait for others to motivate you, you'll be inconsistent in your efforts to reach your goals. If you leave your destiny to others, you will be a victim. People with victim mentality are not self-reliant, and many die unfulfilled, still in the "wait" mode. They wait for their ship to come in. They wait to win the lottery. They wait for perfection. They wait for others to change or to do this or that. Some people become involved "romantically" (if you can call it that) while waiting for that very person to change, and their own self-reliance and fate become sealed in a cocoon of self-neglect. You can't change other people, you can only change yourself. I wish I could write that in ten-foot letters: YOU CAN'T CHANGE OTHER PEOPLE, YOU CAN ONLY CHANGE YOURSELF.

In Ralph Waldo Emerson's essay, Self-Reliance, he says, "Power in nature is the essential measure of right. Nature suffers nothing to remain in her kingdom, which cannot help itself. The genesis and maturation of a planet, its poise and orbit, the bended tree recovering itself from the strong wind, the vital resources of every animal and vegetable, are demonstrations of the self-sufficing, and therefore self-relying, soul."

I believe this is profound. Someone else once said, "Success is not measured in the highs, but how quickly you pick yourself up from the lows." Emerson is telling us that our very lives depend on being able to recover.

118

If we can't be self-reliant enough to bounce back from the storms of life and try again, we will not survive—maybe even literally. We must keep our bootstraps strong and in good repair. They must be at the ready to pull on at any given moment and we must remain tenacious through the pull.

Self-reliance is the only road to true freedom, and being one's own person is its ultimate reward.
~~Patricia Sampson
Author of A Star to Steer By

And, just as you can't do the work for someone else, no one is going to do the work for you. Other people can spur you on, give you ideas, share information, and even show you the way, but the work to become free from external control has to come from you. Otherwise, you wouldn't really be self-reliant, would you?

Part of the work and one of the first steps in learning to be autonomous is establishing and following a values system, as mentioned earlier. This gives you a map to help you stay on track, points you in the direction you want to go, and keeps you from pursuing a path that is detrimental to you and what you want to achieve. A strong set of morale principles will also keep you from relying on people who don't *share* your values—people you don't need in your life.

Learn to find resources on your own. Many years ago I had two aunts. Both were poor and looked to me to help them find health care, benefits and housing. Whenever they approached me to help them, it seemed like they were totally helpless, that there was absolutely no resource that provided what they needed, and that there was no way to find help even if it was out there. So I would search. Eventually, I would come up with answers and resources.

Both of them were amazed at the results. Trust me, I did nothing unusual. I had no magic tricks up my sleeve, I did not have connections in high places, and in the beginning of those searches, I knew probably even less than they did. Finding resources by yourself may include enlisting the help of others. That's OK. Just remember that you may not always get the answer you're looking for. When either of my aunts would be told "No," or "I don't know," or "We can't help you with that," or "That's not our department," they would give up totally defeated and think it was the end.

You can't do that, you must learn to probe for additional information. If the person you ask doesn't know the answer, ask them who does or who they think *might* know the answer. Ask if they know of a source you might investigate. Then follow up with those sources. Learn to use the Internet to search for answers. Find and read books by qualified authors on the topics you need to pursue. Libraries and librarians are a great place to begin. Learn what your rights are in a given situation. Learn to use public information that is (usually) free and available to everyone. The government puts out more information on more topics than you can imagine. Learn to network. Go back to school if necessary.

Even learning how to use positive self-talk is being self-reliant. Your support group may not be physically available when things go wrong, so learning to talk yourself through the tough events and giving yourself encouragement to get to the next step helps you to rely on your own initiative.

Often people say to me, "I've always wanted to do such and such."

My reply is usually, "So why don't you?"

Their comeback is, "I wouldn't know where to start."

This would be a great excuse for someone who has been living in a cave and cut off from civilization. If these people are too lazy to go to the Internet and type in their topic, or go to the library and find a book, they probably don't *want* to do anything. Taking that first step is part of being self-reliant. Without it, your journey to self-fulfillment can't begin. The first step might be doing some research, or joining an organization, or interviewing someone who has already accomplished what you want to accomplish, or simply writing down your goals. There are a number of ways to take that first step, but you are the one who has to take it. No one can do that for you.

A journey of a thousand miles starts with a single step.
~~Chinese proverb

Some people avoid that first step because they look at the end result and not at the steps in between, so they become overwhelmed. But what many fail to realize is that, once the journey begins, the laws of attraction kick in. You will attract the resources and people you need. Jeez, even instant pudding takes some steps to complete.

While I have advised you to break free of habits that are not good for you, being consistent in your pursuit of excellence and positive living is part of being self-reliant and building a better life for yourself. This quote says it beautifully!

Make good habits and they will make you.
~~ Mac Anderson
Founder of Successories, Inc.

"Consistent" is different from "persistent." Being *consistent* means doing the things you say you will do. Being *persistent* means keeping on keeping on. When you are consistent, people know you are in for the long haul and will get the job done. People look for uniformity when they need someone to speak at a meeting, when they need to purchase an important item, and when they need help. Be unchanging in the quality of life you live, in the quality of products or service you deliver, in the quality of friendship you offer.

You have to persevere. You have to do it. I have insecurities. But whatever I'm insecure about, I don't dissect it, but I'll go after it and say, "What am I afraid of?" I bet the average successful person can tell you they've failed much more than they've had success. I've had far more failures than I've had successes. With every commercial I've gotten, there were 200 I didn't get. You have to go after what you're afraid of.

~~Kevin Sorbo (1958)
American actor

An often-overlooked feature of self-reliance is self-promotion. Yes, I mean blowing your own horn! Letting others know about your goals and dreams will help them help you. Yes, I hear you: "Wait a minute, you told me to be self-reliant, now you're telling me to get help from others. What gives?"

The aunt who raised me would often comment, "Oh, Lordy, you just can't depend on other people." She repeated the statement so often that it made quite an impression on me—a negative impression. Being the "all or nothing" person I was, I went to the opposite extreme and never asked for anyone's help, which is not a good thing. Other people can be a great resource and they can keep you motivated (see Step Three: Get a Support System). The following excerpts from Ralph Waldo Emerson's essay, *Self-Reliance,* explain it beautifully, and his ideas are just as meaningful today:

A man [I'm not sure what Emerson had in mind here, but let's assume he meant humankind] should learn to detect and watch that gleam of light which flashes across his mind from within, more than the luster of the firmament of bards and sages. Yet he dismisses without notice his thought, because it is his. In every work of genius, we recognize our own rejected thoughts; they come back to us with a certain alienated majesty. Great works of art have no more affecting lesson for us than this: They teach us to abide by our spontaneous impression with good-humored inflexibility most when the whole cry of voices is on the other side. Else, tomorrow a stranger will say with masterly good sense precisely what we have thought and felt all the time, and we shall be forced to take with shame our own opinion from another.

How many times have you heard someone say about a new invention, "I had that idea a year ago; why didn't I pursue it?" Learn to detect and watch those gleams. We all have them.

A man is to carry himself in the presence of all opposition as if everything were titular and ephemeral but him. I am ashamed to think how easily we capitulate to badges and names, to large societies and dead institutions.

Face challenges one by one, one step at a time, and keep moving forward.

123

What I must do is all that concerns me, not what the people think. This rule, equally arduous in actual and in intellectual life, may serve for the whole distinction between greatness and meanness. It is the harder, because you will always find those who think they know your duty better than you know it. It is easy in the world to live after the world's opinion; it is easy in solitude to live after our own; but the great man is he who in the mindset of the crowd keeps with perfect sweetness the independence of solitude.

Be yourself and do what you love!

The objection to conforming to usages that have become dead to you is that it scatters your force. It loses your time and blurs the impression of your character.

Don't cling to habits, people or routines that no longer benefit you and your goals. While this may sound Machiavellian (the idea that any means justify the end), you become what you read and who you associate with in life.

The other terror that scares us from self-trust is our consistency, a reverence for our past act or word, because the eyes of others have no other data for computing our orbit than our past acts, and we are loath to disappoint them.

We sometimes do things because others expect it of us. We find it difficult to renege on our routines, even when they are destructive, because we don't want to disappoint others. You are the one who must not be disappointed at life's end.

But why should you keep your head over your shoulder? Why drag about this corpse of your memory, lest you contradict something you have stated in this or that public place? Suppose you should contradict yourself—what then? It seems to be a rule of wisdom never to rely on your memory alone, into the thousand-eyed present, and live ever in a new day. In your metaphysics, you have denied personality to the Deity. Yet when the devout motions of the soul come, you yield to them heart and life, though they should clothe God with shape and color. Leave your theory, as Joseph left his coat in the hand of the harlot, and flee.

The voyage of the best ship is a zigzag line of a hundred tacks. See the line from a sufficient distance and it straightens itself to the average tendency. Your genuine action will explain itself, and will explain your other genuine actions. Your conformity explains nothing. Act singly, and what you have already done singly will justify you now. Greatness appeals to the future. If I can be firm enough today to do right, and scorn eyes, I must have done so much right before as to defend me now. Be it how it will, do right now. Always scorn appearances, and you always may. The force of character is cumulative. All the foregone days of virtue work their health into this.

One person—each of us—has the power to make a difference in the world. Your bootstraps are elastic—they will help you reach new heights.

Let a man then know his worth, and keep things under his feet. Let him not peep or steal, or skulk up and down with the air of a charity-boy, a bastard, or an interloper, in the world which exists for him. But the man in the street, finding no worth in himself which corresponds to the force which built a tower or sculptured a marble god, feels poor when he looks on these. To him a palace, a statue, or a costly book have an alien and forbidding air, much like a gay equipage, and seem to say, "Who are you, Sir?" Yet they all are his—suitors for his notice, petitioners to his faculties, that they will come out and take possession. The picture waits for my verdict: it is not to command me, but I am to settle its claims to praise. That popular fable of the sot who was picked up dead drunk in the street, carried to the duke's house, washed and dressed and laid in the duke's bed, and, on his waking, treated with all obsequious ceremony like the duke and assured that he had been insane, owes its popularity to the fact that it symbolizes so well the state of man, who is in the world a sort of sot, but now and then wakes up, exercises his reason, and find himself a true prince.

No one and nothing is better than you; we are all true princes.

The magnetism which all original action exerts is explained when we inquire the reason of self-trust. Who is the Trustee? What is the aboriginal Self on which a universal reliance may be grounded? What is the nature and power of that science-baffling star, without parallax, without calculable elements, which shoots a ray of beauty even into trivial and impure actions if the least mark of independence appears? The inquiry leads us to that source, at once the essence of genius, of virtue, and of life, which we call Spontaneity or Instinct. We denote this primary wisdom's Intuition, whilst all later teachings are tuitions.

It isn't that we don't have intuition. We do, and we all have at least a little engraved in the DNA of our bootstraps. But some of us don't listen to it or even allow it to speak loudly enough to be heard. More often than not, we don't even give it *time* to speak before we make the next knee-jerk decision. Typically, such decisions are not our best ones. Learning to trust and develop your intuition will pave the way for self-reliance. Here are six steps to help your intuition play a more predominant role in your life:

(1) Focus. Don't let your thoughts be distracted. Pay attention to what is happening in the now.

(2) Trust that you do have intuition and allow it to speak to you. Listen when it does.

(3) Keep a journal, or at least find a way to take some time out for yourself each day. Try meditation or prayer.

(4) Know and understand how you feel physically and emotionally in both good and bad times. This will help you understand which of your thoughts and actions are driven by feelings and emotions. Keep everything in logical perspective.

(5) Understand what events and steps need to occur in what order. For example, you can't become a teacher until you go to college and earn a degree. You can't enter college until you have completed high school requirements. Life, too, has events that usually work out best when taken in order. Take my daughter. (PLEASE! Just kidding.) She quit school, got pregnant, got married, got divorced, got her GED and then went to college. While she certainly survived all of this, her life would have been much smoother had she taken things in order: high school, college, marriage, pregnancy and then parenthood. Life is complicated enough without adding to the chaos.

(6) Learn from mistakes and look at them as learning opportunities. Don't forget to look at what went right and build on those things.

Now, back to Emerson:

In that deep force, the last fact behind which analysis cannot go, all things find their common origin. For the sense of being, which in calm hours rises... in the soul, is not diverse from things, from space, from light, from time, from man, but is one with them, and proceeds obviously from the same source whence their life and being also proceed. We first share life by which things exist, and afterwards see them as appearances in nature and forget that we have shared their cause. Here is the fountain of action and of thought. Here are the lungs of that inspiration which giveth man wisdom, and which cannot be denied without impiety and atheism. We lie in the lap of immense intelligence, which makes us receivers of its truth and organs of its activity. When we discern justice, when we discern truth, we do nothing of ourselves, but allow a passage to its beams. If we ask whence this comes, if we seek to pry into the soul that causes, all philosophy is at fault. Its presence or its absence is all we can affirm. Every man discriminates between the voluntary acts of his mind and his involuntary perceptions, and knows that to his involuntary perceptions a perfect faith is due. He may err in the expression of them, but he knows that these things are so like day and night as not to be disputed. My willful actions and acquisitions are but roving: the idlest reverie, the faintest native emotion, commands my curiosity and respect. Thoughtless people contradict as readily the statement of perceptions as of opinions, or rather much more readily; for they do not distinguish between perception and notion. They fancy that I choose to see this or that thing. But perception is not whimsical but fatal. If I see a trait, my children will see it after me, and in course of time, all mankind, although it may chance that no one has seen it before me. For my perception of it is as much a fact as the sun.

Today, we say that perception is reality. It is vitally important that your self-perception be realistic and honest. But that perception must be laced with appreciation and the courage to change the negative.

Man is timid and apologetic; he is no longer upright; he dares not say, "I think," "I am," but quotes some saint or sage. He is ashamed before the blade of grass or the blowing rose. These roses under my window make no reference to former roses or to better ones; they are for what they are; they exist with God today. There is no time to them. There is simply the rose; it is perfect in every moment of its existence. Before a leaf-bud has burst, its whole life acts. In the full-blown flower there is no more; in the leafless root there is no less. Its nature is satisfied, and it satisfies nature, in all moments alike. But man postpones or remembers; he does not live in the present, but with reverted eye laments the past, or, heedless of the riches that surround him, stands on tiptoe to foresee the future. He cannot be happy and strong until he too lives with nature in the present, above time.

If we cannot at once rise to the sanctities of obedience and faith, let us at least resist our temptations. Let us enter into the state of war and wake Thor and Woden, courage and constance, in our Saxon breasts. This is to be done in our smooth times by speaking the truth. Check this lying hospitality and lying affection. Live no longer to the expectation of these deceived and deceiving people with whom we converse. Say to them, "O father, O mother, O wife, O brother, O friend, I have lived with you after appearances hitherto. Henceforward I am the truth's. Be it known unto you that henceforward I obey no law less than the eternal law. I will have no covenants but proximities. I shall endeavor to nourish my parents, to support my family, to be the chaste husband of one wife [or the chaste wife of one husband], but these relations I must fill after a new and unprecedented way. I appeal from your customs. I must be myself. I cannot break myself any longer for you. If you can love me for what I am, we shall be the happier. If you cannot, I will still seek to deserve that you should. I will not hide my tastes or aversions. I will so trust that what is deep is holy, that I will do strongly before the sun and moon whatever only rejoices me, and the heart appoints. If you are noble, I will love you; if you are not, I will not hurt you and myself by hypocritical attentions. If you are true, but not in the same truth with me, cleave to your compan- ions; I will seek my own. I do this not selfishly, but humbly and truly. It is [in] your interest and mine, and all men's, however long we have dwelt in lies, to live in truth. Does this sound harsh today? You will soon love what is dictated by your nature as well as mine, and if we follow the truth, it will bring us out safe at last."

But so you may give these friends pain. Yes, but I cannot sell my liberty and my power to save their sensibility. Besides, all persons have their moments of reason, when they look out into the region of absolute truth. Then will they justify me, and do the same thing.

Just because someone is a relative does not give them the right to hold you back, treat you unkindly or make you live your life to please them. You must dispatch negative people from your life. I have a close relative I have chosen not to associate with because he brings trouble and turmoil to my life. I have my own troubles and turmoil, thank you. I love the sentence above: "If you are noble, I will love you; if you are not, I will not hurt you and myself by hypocritical attentions." Emerson's use of the word "noble" here has nothing to do with being of high birth—it refers to being of superior character. Those who would hurt you, emotionally or physically, are not noble. Those who deny your right to fulfill your dreams are not noble. Get these people out of your life NOW! You don't need them now, nor will you ever need them, in order to be yourself or achieve your goals.

If our young men miscarry in their first enterprise, they lose all heart. If the young merchant fails, men say he is ruined. If the finest genius studies at one of our colleges and is not installed in an office within one year afterwards in the cities or suburbs of Boston or New York, it seems to his friends and to himself that he is right in being disheartened, and in complaining the rest of his life.

We've all seen bitter people like this.

A sturdy lad [or lassie] from New Hampshire or Vermont, who in turn tries all the professions, who teams it, farms it, peddles, keeps a school, preaches, edits a newspaper, goes to Congress, buys a township, and so forth, in successive years, and always, like a cat, falls on his feet, is worth a hundred of these city dolls. He walks abreast with his days, and feels no shame in not "studying a profession," for he does not postpone his life, but lives already. He has not one chance, but a hundred chances.

Opportunities are like buses: if you miss one, another will be along soon.

Let a Stoic open the resources of man, and tell men they are not leaning willows but can and must detach themselves; that with the exercise of self-trust, new powers shall appear; that a man is the word made flesh, born to shed healing to the nations that he should be ashamed of our compassion; and that the moment he acts from himself, tossing the laws, books, idolatries, and customs out of the window, we pity him no more, but thank and revere him, and that teacher shall restore the life of man to splendor, and make his name dear to all history. It is easy to see that a greater self-reliance must work a revolution in all the offices and relations of me, in their religion, their education, their pursuits, their modes of living, their association, their property, their speculative views.

This passage reminds me of those who say, "God will provide." I put more stock in the saying "God helps those who help themselves." A few months ago, I was in the Atlanta airport waiting for a flight. I overheard a man and woman talking. The woman said, "I don't believe in heaven or hell. I believe *this* is hell." Now there's an excuse that's hard to beat!

She was saying, "I'm living in hell; I'm already beaten. There is no reason to grow or to make life better, because this life is hell and I can only give up and suffer through it." That woman is doing something w-r-o-n-g! Her attitude is self-defeatism and in direct opposition to self-reliance. She doesn't have to bother doing anything more until death comes to claim her and take her away from this hell. Why bother? People like her definitely need a "revolution in their modes of living."

When you begin to think and talk in terms of *possibilities* instead of *impossibilities,* you will see life and the opportunities it presents. When you think and talk in terms of "Can do!" instead of "Why try?" you will find courage you never knew you had.

This passage also brings to mind people who use the mantra "I'm waiting for God to tell me what to do with my life." I prefer the mantra "God helps those who help themselves." Here's the difference: Both of these statements send a subliminal message to your unconscious. Remember that the unconscious mind doesn't know truth from fiction or fact from fallacy. It acts on whatever message you send it. The first statement above almost gives you permission to lie back and let life pass you by. The second gives you permission to take control and go after whatever you want. Emerson nails it in the next quote:

Another sort of false prayers are our regrets. Discontent is the want of self-reliance: it is infirmity of will.

The woman in the airport's will is infirm and sick—very much in need of therapy, self-love and vision.

The secret of fortune is joy in our hands. Welcome evermore to gods and men is the self-helping man. For him all doors are flung wide, all tongues greet, all honors crown, all eyes follow with desire. Our love goes out to him and embraces him because he did not need it.

This is sort of like the rule that banks only lend money to those who don't need it!

We solicitously and apologetically caress and celebrate him, because he held on his way and scorned our disapprobation. The gods love him because men hated him. "To the persevering mortal," said Zoroaster, "the blessed Immortals are swift." He who knows that power is inborn, that he is weak because he has looked for good out of him and elsewhere, and so perceiving, throws himself unhesitatingly on his thought, instantly rights himself, stands in the erect position, commands his limbs, works miracles; just as a man who stands on his feet is stronger than a man who stands on his head.

Here is a more modern interpretation from the song "You Gotta Be" by Des'ree, Epic/550 Music, 1994:

"You gotta be. You gotta be bad, you gotta be bold, you gotta be wiser. You gotta be hard, you gotta be tough, you gotta be stronger. You gotta be cool, you gotta be calm, you gotta stay together. All I know, all I know, is that love will save the day."

Just remember that the love has to begin with loving yourself and your own spirit.

A political victory, a rise of rents, the recovery of your sick, the return of your absent friend, or some other favorable event, raises your spirits and you think goods days are preparing for you. Do not believe it. Nothing can bring you peace but yourself. Nothing can bring you peace but the triumph of principles.

I couldn't have said it better myself! If you want to read Emerson's essay in its entirety, go to http://rwe.org/works/Essays-1st_Series_02_Self-Reliance.htm.

You are a child of God. Your playing small does not serve the world. There is nothing enlightened about shrinking so that other people won't feel insecure about you. We were born to manifest the glory of God that is within us.

~~Nelson Mandela (1918)
Former South African president

You mean you didn't know that your bootstraps
glow in the dark?

And as we let our own light shine, we unconsciously give other people permission to do the same. As we are liberated from our own fear, our presence automatically liberates others.

~~Nelson Mandela, ibid.

Hey, does Mandela have that light thing down or what?
Remember that what goes around comes around.

Always look at what you have left. Never look at what you have lost.

~~Robert H. Schuller, ibid.

If it's to be, it's up to me!

~~William H. Johnsen

No one can cheat you out of ultimate success but yourself.

~~Ralph Waldo Emerson, ibid

Depend not on another, but lean instead on thyself.
True happiness is born of self-reliance.
~~From "The Laws of Manu" (1500 BCE)
Central text of Hinduism

WARNING! If this quote makes you think you should never ask for help with those bootstraps, think again. No one on this planet achieves success as an island. Asking for help in coloring, straightening, pulling or building your bootstraps is a true sign of maturity.

No man is an island entire of itself; every man is a piece of the continent, a part of the main.
~~John Donne (1572-1632)
British poet

Step 11: Do It Now—Go for the Gusto!

At the age of 56, it hit me like a ton of bricks, like a wet salmon being slapped across my face, like someone had just screamed in my ear, "Wake the hell up!" I had come to the realization that, within four years, I would be 60! In fact, the original title of this book was *Suddenly Sixty*. What happened to all those years? Well, of course, the years between 1 and 56 were there, but where was *I*? What did I *do* during all those years?

Quite frankly, I screwed up a lot of them. But I have decided that I don't want to screw up the years I have left. I guess I'll always be subject to making poor decisions, but I need to keep the batting average on the high side. And so do you. It's never too late to begin making the best decisions for your life, regardless of the number of candles on your birthday cake. (Seems like people spend more time deciding what movie to rent than they do designing a life that will give them fulfillment and serenity.) Remember: The early bird may get the worm, but the second mouse gets the cheese. I'm going for the cheese, er, I mean the gusto. I've enrolled in school. I'm going back, and this time, my major is going to be psychology. Wish me luck, I think I'll need it!

My mother was not the best mother in the world, but she was a beautiful, talented, witty and charming individual. She could sew and crochet like nobody's business. But she never had the courage to use her wonderful attributes to make her life worth living. For the most part, her life was quite unhappy—even desperate at times, I imagine. I took care of her in the last few months of her terminal cancer. Shortly after she came to my home, she said,

"This is the happiest I've ever been, lying here on my death bed."

Don't let those be the words to describe your life. When we're young, we find it difficult to think of limited days or how we will fill the time between birth and death. Then suddenly we find that the time has zipped past us and we have failed to design, build and live the life we wanted. For some, it's too late, but not for you. (I'm making the assumption that you are still breathing if you're reading this!) Find the thing you want to do and do it as well as you possibly can.

How? Rob E. Geraghty, phobia expert, says, "The answer is going out and *doing* rather than waiting. If you wait, life will probably pass you by. But if you go and do the things you want to do, take the risks you fear, you may just find that everything slots into place."

I heard a phrase not too long ago that pretty well captures my philosophy of life:

"If you aren't living on the edge, you're taking up too much space." It has nothing to do with thrill-seeking. It's about making the most of every moment, about stretching your own boundaries, about being willing to learn constantly and putting yourself in situations where learning is possible—sometimes even critical to your survival. Being out on the edge, with everything at risk, is where you learn— and grow—the most.
~~ Jim Whitaker (1929) Mountaineer, adventurer, speaker, environmentalist
From his book, A Life on the Edge:
Memoirs of Everest and Beyond

If your boundaries are not that far "out there," that's all the more reason to begin now to build the future you want. Decide what you want to accomplish and begin building it step by step. Seek out your life's adventures.

My colleague, Jon Schwartz, plays a character named Vinny Verelli (www.motivatethis.net). Vinny's favorite slogan is "Get off your butt and do something." And Nike has sold millions of shoes with the marketing slogan, "Just do it!" So that's what I'm telling you: Go do something!

It is not death that a man should fear; he should fear never beginning to live.
~~Marcus Aelius Aurelius (121-180 AD)
Roman emperor and philosopher

Adventure isn't hanging on a rope off the side of a mountain. Adventure is an attitude that we must apply to the day-to-day obstacles of life—facing new challenges, seizing new opportunities, testing our resources against the unknown and, in the process, discovering our own unique potential.
~~John Amatt (1945)
Organizer and participant in Canada's first successful expedition to the summit of Mount Everest

---

Yes! Our everyday lives are an adventure. If you want to succeed, you must have this optimistic attitude of life as a journey to be taken, a process to be enjoyed, a situation to be relished. Recently I overheard some people making fun of a member of their family because she had turned 30. She suffered a barrage of "over the hill" jabs and jibes. She tried to take them in a lighthearted manner, but I could see the pained expression behind her smiles of endurance. As someone wise once said, old age is a privilege denied to many. Managing the seasons of our lives is like creating a work of art for ourselves and those around us. We know, in generalities, what each of life's seasons brings us, so why not anticipate the joys of each and prepare to paint them in vivid colors? Regrets would then be nonexistent.

Life moves on, whether we act as cowards or heroes.
~~Henry Miller (1891-1980)
American writer

Make the most of yourself, for that is all there is of you.
~~Ralph Waldo Emerson, ibid.

Summary

You must—for the life of you and your loved ones—you must stop being a victim and find your own bootstraps.

Here's a reminder of the 11 steps outlined in this book:

Step 1: Get to Know Yourself. Being able to look inward and examine yourself—to understand what you value and who you are—is the first step toward a successful and happy life. People who are unable to be alone with themselves never become acquainted with their own best friend. People who run from conflict and confrontation never know what they stand for or how much they can bear. Those who don't know their strengths and weaknesses never know who or what they need to incorporate or leave out of their lives to reach success.

Step 2: Use Positive Self-Talk. To be successful, you must tear down any negative foundation and build a new, more positive foundation. This step costs you nothing, it's something you can do every single day, you can start it any time, you will also learn how to incorporate accountability into other areas of your (life like self-worth and well-being), and it works miracles for your growth.

Positive self-talk will also help you become your own person. Letting others decide what your life should be like is no life at all. Ask yourself what YOU want.

Step 3: Get a Support System. Meet new people. Hire a coach. Learn to network. Choose dependable friends.

Step 4: Find Your Passion. Think back to your childhood. What did you pretend to be? What did you daydream about when you were alone and free to concentrate on your favorite thoughts? What excited you about those thoughts? What made you feel whole or real or satisfied with yourself? That is your true passion.

Step 5: Embrace Error Messages. Change makes up our lives—it happens every day. People are born, die, make money, file for bankruptcy, get married, get divorced, start a new job, get fired or quit. Buildings are built and are torn down. New companies are formed, others fold. The boss you had yesterday goes to work at another company today, and on and on and on. All of these events create change, and mistakes are made, but the planet keeps turning no matter who makes what mistake.

Step 6: Fight the Fear Factor. Clearly identify the fear you want to conquer. Analyze why you have this fear. Prepare. Study other people doing what you fear, especially those you want to emulate. Use positive visualization. Do what you fear at every opportunity.

Step 7: Give up Guilt. Buying into guilt is a losing proposition. You lose your energy, time and personal power. Don't let a spouse, parent or member of society make you feel guilty for trying to change your life. You don't need to carry around someone else's perceptions of guilt. Don't be afraid to tell others No. This one idea alone will save you countless hours of worry and give you more time.

Step 8: Be Persistent. You must have purpose, desire, self- reliance, a precise plan, accurate knowledge, cooperation, willpower, good habits and follow-up.

Step 9: Build Your Self-Esteem: Be yourself. Learn to recognize and appreciate your every asset. Don't compare yourself to others. Use what you have. Invest in yourself every day by doing at least one thing toward your goals.

Step 10: Become Self-Reliant. You can't change other people, you can only change yourself. Benjamin Franklin told us that it takes only 21 days to develop a new habit, and today's behavioralists confirm it. What is your first positive habit going to be?

Step 11: Do It Now. When we're young, we find it difficult to think of life's end or how we will fill the time between birth and death. Then suddenly we find that our days have zipped past us and we have failed to design, build and live the life we wanted. For some, it's too late, but not for you. Find the thing you want to do and do it as well as you possibly can.

Keep your bootstraps handy, folks! When you begin this wonderful journey, you're gonna need something to hang on to!

Stretching Your Bootstraps and Moving Your Life Forward!

If you're really serious about overcoming victim thinking, getting your life together, reaching your goals and being self-reliant, consider coaching with Diane. For more information, send an email to diane@performstrat.com Be sure to put I WANT TO MOVE FORWARD in the subject line.

Order Additional Copies of "Boots" and Other Books by Diane

Finding Your Bootstraps: 11 Steps to Overcoming Victim Thinking - **$14.75**

Number of copies: _____

There's Something Funny about Humor in Presentations - **$10.00**

Number of copies: _____

Secrets of Writing a *Winning Resume so You Get the Job You Want* ebook
http://www.amazon.com/dp/B00AV9X8HM - **$17.95**

By Mail: 2312 Clairmont Road NE, Atlanta, GA 30329
Make check or money order payable to: *Performance Strategies, Inc*

By Fax: 404-736-6090

By Phone: 404.320.7834
To pay with a credit card visit the website:
http:findingyourbootstraps.com

Please send me info on:

☐ Diane's speaking programs

☐ Assessments

☐ Coaching (Business/Life/Career)

☐ Think and Grow Rich by the Numbers Workshop
